MODERN MILITARY SERIES

TANKS

MODERN MILITARY SERIES
Editor Michael Leitch

TANKS

by Eric Morris

Introduction by Aram Bakshian, Jr.

Octopus
Octopus Books

JACKET FRONT *Britain's most up-to-date tank, the Chieftain, displays its deadly 120-mm main armament.*

JACKET BACK *The American Sherman tank, an 'old regular', makes an appearance in the Arab–Israeli War of 1967.*

PAGE 1 *An Israeli tank moves swiftly into battle.*

PREVIOUS PAGES *Knocked-out Arab tanks during the Middle-East conflict.*

THIS PAGE *A Crusader Mk I in the desert campaign of 1942.*

First published in 1975 by Octopus Books Limited, 59 Grosvenor Street, London W.1.
ISBN 0 7064 0301 0
© 1975 Octopus Books Limited
Distributed in Australia by Rigby Limited, 30 North Terrace, Kent-Town, Adelaide, South Australia 5067
Produced by Mandarin Publishers Limited, 14 Westlands Road, Quarry Bay, Hong Kong
Printed in Hong Kong.

Contents

ANATOMY OF A TANK

These illustrations are intended to show the principal components of a main battle tank. The shape and performance of tanks has undergone many radical changes since the first of the breed went into action on the Somme in 1916. Even so, the principle of a gunned and armoured obstacle-crossing vehicle has remained more or less constant. As our representative tank we feature the German Pzkw Mark VI Tiger 1, first used on active service in September 1942 on the Leningrad front.

RIGHT This front view demonstrates the all-round traversing capabilities of the turret and main gun, and the arc within which the muzzle could be elevated or depressed. Also shown are the driver's vision slit, and the hull machine-gun.

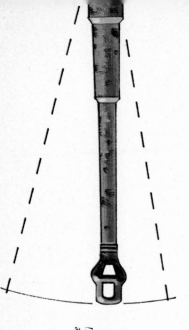

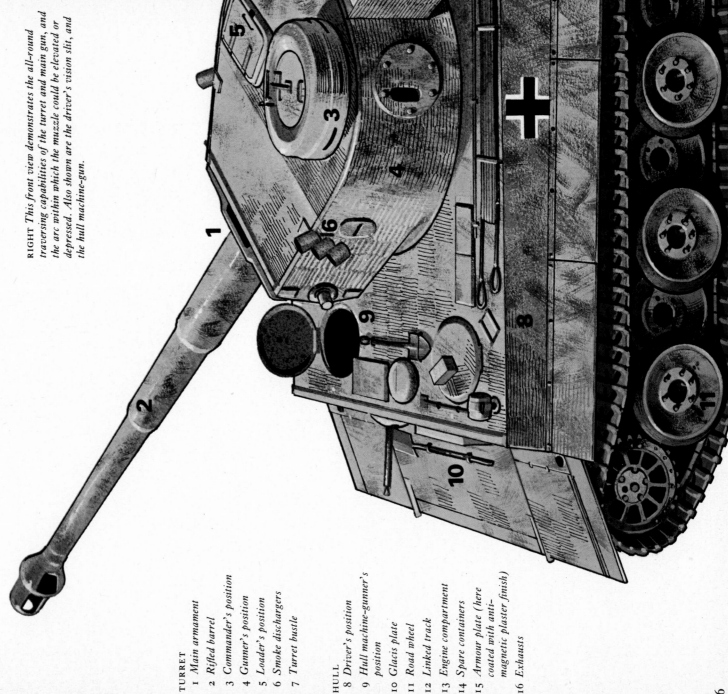

TURRET

1 Main armament
2 Rifled barrel
3 Commander's position
4 Gunner's position
5 Loader's position
6 Smoke dischargers
7 Turret bustle

HULL

8 Driver's position
9 Hull machine-gunner's position
10 Glacis plate
11 Road wheel
12 Linked track
13 Engine compartment
14 Spare containers
15 Armour plate (here coated with anti-magnetic plaster finish)
16 Exhausts

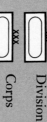

KEY TO SYMBOLS USED IN MAPS

SYMBOL	MEANING	SPECIFIC MEANING OF EXAMPLE
1 Infantry Formations		
x	Brigade or regiment	
xx	Division	
xxx Fr IV	Corps	French Fourth Corps
xxxx US THIRD Patton	Army	US Third Army commanded by General Patton
xxxxx 21 Montgomery	Army Group	Twenty-first Army Group commanded by General Montgomery
2 Armoured Formations		
x	Brigade or regiment	
xx	Division	
xxx Pz XV Hoth	Corps	Fifteenth Panzer Corps commanded by General Hoth
xxxx Pz Group II Guderian	Panzer Group	Second Panzer Group commanded by General Guderian
xxxx SIXTH Dietrich	Army	Sixth Panzer Army commanded by General Dietrich
3 Boundaries		
— xxx —	Corps boundary	
— xxxx —	Army boundary	
— xxxxx —	Army group boundary	
4 Commands		
SHAEF Eisenhower	Supreme Command	Supreme Head-quarters Allied Expeditionary Forces commanded by General Eisenhower
OB WEST von Rundstedt	High Command	Hitler's Western High Command led by Field-Marshal von Rundstedt

Veteran Sherman tanks on the desert trail, line ahead.

Introduction

by Aram Bakshian, Jr

The tank – is it one of the shortest-lived wonders of military history, destined to dominate the battlefield for a short period and then slowly settle back into obscurity and obsolescence? This much is certain: its high point as the offensive core of major armies was reached in World War II. It is unlikely that our generation or any future one will ever again witness the spectacle of massed tanks clanking into a European battle like some latterday version of Napoleon's iron-clad heavy cavalry.

Yet on the fringes of multi-national conflict, in the deserts of the Middle East and in military 'police actions' such as the Soviet suppression of Czechoslovakia in 1968, the role of the tank has remained a critical one. Ironic echoes of Rommel's desert raiders could be sensed in the lightning strikes of Israeli tank forces in the Six Day War in 1967, a blitzkrieg that succeeded against a backward enemy who attempted to use his tanks as static defensive weapons rather than as modern battle cavalry. In 1973 the Arab armies used their tanks more aggressively and showed a far greater appreciation of battlefield tactics.

Certainly, as a visible manifestation of overwhelming physical force, the tank was supremely effective in the streets of occupied Prague, where the futile efforts of an unarmed civilian population against the material might of Soviet armour were doomed to fail. There the tank served not as a battlefield tool but as a political one – a means of coercing the civilian population and reasserting domination over a satellite state. This tank role, unlike the other, is likely to increase rather than decrease in the years ahead as dissidence continues behind the Iron Curtain and as the chronic instability of many Asian, Latin American

and African states continues to prompt military coups. Actions of that type nevertheless seem small compared to the days when a Rommel, a Patton or a Montgomery could swing the balance of history with an armoured assault. Yet, in an age when war seems destined to be fought within severely limited bounds, or simultaneously begun and ended in a series of mushroom clouds, such a diminution in stature is perhaps inevitable.

Like Hannibal's elephants, the war chariots of antiquity, the armoured battle wagons of the great 15th-century Bohemian warrior, Jan Ziska, and the dashing 'horse cavalry' of more recent memory, the modern tank is slowly lumbering out of the martial limelight after a starring role of little more than half a century.

But in that half century we may clearly see how much the balance of global power has been affected by the clash of armour. It is a story well worth the telling, and Eric Morris in this opening title of the Octopus Modern Military Series, has told it to perfection. In words and pictures he has gathered it together, from the muddy, blood-soaked trenches of World War I down to the recent armoured battles of Arab and Israeli, Indian and Pakistani.

Today, with the development of a wide range of sophisticated anti-tank weapons, not to mention tactical nuclear weapons, there is no such thing as an invulnerable tank. But tanks by the thousand continue to occupy a large part of every major arsenal in the world, and this is a situation we can expect to continue far into the future. Although the mystique of tanks may have faded and their importance dwindled somewhat, it will be a long time before mankind sees the last of these fascinating and lethal iron horses of war.

The modern battle tank traces its lineage back to the Western Front of 1916, when it was created to meet the specific needs of that battlefield. But as a concept the tank embraces the same principles of mobility, protection and offensive power that have influenced combat since the beginning of organized warfare.

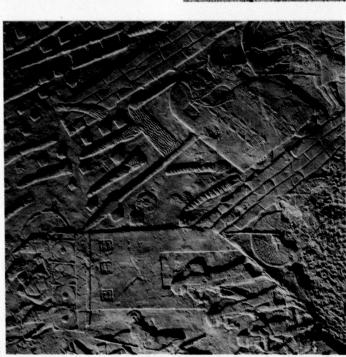

THIS PAGE *Assyrian engines of war, in the ninth–seventh centuries BC, included the turreted ram (above); as the defenders flung down lighted torches, the Assyrians countered by pouring water onto their machine from a long-armed ladle. Other machines were the war chariot (above right) used for carrying attacks at speed to the enemy, and the long, low ram with front turret (below right).*

OPPOSITE *These pre-1914 cards demonstrate various ways in which cavalry brought mobility and the offensive power of firearm and cold steel to the battlefield – until it was finally rendered obsolete by the rapid-firing weapons of the Industrial Revolution. The cavalrymen shown range chronologically from a Private Gentleman of His Majesty's Own Troop of Guards, 1660 (top left) to a Trooper in the 1st Life Guards Camel Corps, 1884–85 (bottom right).*

Private Gentleman of the 1st (or His Majesty's Own) Troop of Guards, 1660.

The Royal Regt of Scots Dragoons, 1681.

Trooper, Horse Grenadiers, 1742.

Trooper, Light Dragoons, 1775.

Sergeant, 10th Light Dragoons (hussars) 1815.

Officer, Life Guards, 1854.

Trooper, 2nd (Royal North British) Dragoons 1854.

Trooper, 17th Lancers, 1854.

Officer, 10th Hussars 1876-80.

Trooper, 1st Life Guards, Levée, 1884-5.

Many ancient peoples made use of war chariots and armoured horsemen to carry an attack to an enemy at speed, while at the same time equipping their warriors with some degree of protection. The armoured elephants of Hannibal and Kublai Khan were variations of this concept, the chief difference in their case being that they were founded on elephant power, whereas war chariots and most forms of armoured cavalry depended on horse power. The tank, on the other hand, differs from every previous form of cavalry or mobile fighting platform in that it runs on mechanical power.

The Function of Cavalry

Throughout history cavalry has had to combine the requirements of mobility, protection and offensive power if it was to make a decisive contribution to the battlefield. When employed as part of a balanced military formation its main duties include observing and reporting information about the enemy; screening movements of its own force; pursuing and demoralizing a defeated enemy; maintaining a constant threat to an enemy's rear area; striking suddenly at any weak spots detected; turning an exposed flank, and exploiting a penetration or break-through.

Vital as these functions are, they nevertheless represent an essentially secondary role to that of the main force. Almost invariably this has been the infantry, and only on rare occasions in its history has the cavalry been able to achieve superiority over the weapons of the defence and so become an arm of decision. This was the case for a brief period when, for example, the Crusader knights – through the quality of their horsemanship and the protection provided by chain-mail – were able to dominate the battlefield.

But later the introduction of the firearm and its gradual improvement between the 14th and 18th centuries placed increasing limitations on the shock value of cavalry.

In the aftermath of the Napoleonic wars came the further development of the rifle and the bullet and then, for the first time, the foot soldier had an efficient and reliable weapon with a range of 1,000 yards; this sealed the doom of the cavalry charge. At the same time rifled and breech-loading field-pieces worked a revolution in artillery tactics, and the revolver and repeating carbines opened up new vistas for the cavalry and rendered obsolete the charge of lancers.

Defence and Concealment

In the American Civil War (1861–65) cavalry tactics entered a period of transition. The battles of this war were dominated by the weapons of the defence, and the rifle and the earthwork were supreme. By 1863 cavalry tactics on both sides had become concerned primarily with dismounted action – which proved so successful that the mounted charge was rarely used. But the wars that occurred in Europe after 1865 were marked by a complete disregard of the cavalry lessons demonstrated in America. The Austro-Prussian War (1866) saw 60,000 horsemen armed with lance and sabre charging in the face of the breech-loading needle-gun and the Minié rifle. In the Franco-Prussian War, just five years later, an even larger force of 100,000 horsemen, similarly armed, was deployed for battle. Both sides attempted the mass charge. The French cavalry, which had learned nothing since Waterloo, was defeated, while the better-trained and more disciplined Prussians succeeded – though at a terrible cost, since by then the French had developed a machine-gun, the *mitrailleuse*. (It is to Von Bredow's Uhlans that the dubious distinction belongs of providing the last successful massed boot-to-boot cavalry charge in military history.)

The Boer farmers of South Africa were frontiersmen in the American tradition and at the beginning of the 20th century they taught the British Army a lesson in mobility and firepower which it has never forgotten. The British infantry was constantly outmanoeuvred by the mounted Boer rifleman, while the cavalry, which insisted on retaining the sabre and the lance, proved equally ineffective. It was not until the British commanders created mounted units, organized on a dragoon basis, and deployed them in overwhelming numbers, that the hardy Boer commanders were defeated.

On the Western Front at the beginning of World War I 10 German cavalry divisions numbering more than 70,000 men faced 10 French and one British division across trenches whose construction they had been powerless to prevent – such were the limitations which the weapons of the defence had by now placed on movement. Nevertheless the opening months of the war provided ample opportunity for cavalry exploitation, but once again the generals failed to see that the need was for mounted riflemen and not the European cavalry of the day – which still relied on the sword and the lance in mounted action.

OPPOSITE *The mitrailleuse, the French built multi-barrelled machine-gun which failed, through faulty deployment, to stop the Prussian cavalry in 1870–71. Its potential was, however, only too clear.*

ABOVE *By the Russo-Japanese War the need for concealment had already produced a new, static kind of warfare. Shown here are Russian artillery trenches and dugouts in a hilltop position defending Port Arthur.*

BELOW *Even in World War 1 the cavalry of Europe foolishly persisted with the sword and lance. These outmoded heroes are Cossacks at the Battle of Tannenberg on the Eastern Front, 1914.*

Machine-guns and gas dulled men's appetites for fighting but the Great War continued. For four winters the armies of the Western Front were sacrificed in exchange for handfuls of ground. John Nash's painting Over the Top *illuminates the drudgery of trench warfare.*

Stalemate in the Trenches

By the spring of 1915 the Western Front had congealed into stagnation. Mobility and manoeuvre, the prime assets of good generalship, had already been displaced by the conflicting demands of static warfare, in which artillery and manpower were most in demand, while the élite regiments of cavalry were relegated to the role of frustrated observers. The quick-firing artillery piece and the machine-gun, together with the trench and barbed wire, had combined together in a grisly yet revolutionary quartet to emphasize what the American Civil War had made clear half a century earlier – and the Russo–Japanese War of 1904–5 had more recently confirmed – namely that through the legacy of the Industrial Revolution warfare had been changed beyond all recognition.

As their next step the commanders on both sides sought to restore mobility and manoeuvre to a stagnant battlefield. At Ypres the British attempted to create an artificial flank by means of a salient and the Germans attempted to seize the initiative through the use of gas; both failed. Thereafter the Germans were content to rest on the defensive while the Allied generals, with the principle of surprise beyond reach, fell back on a solution which reflected their despair. Attrition was now hailed as the way to defeat Germany. Such was the low level of inventiveness among the High Commands of both sides in the year before the tank made its initial fighting appearance at the First Battle of the Somme.

The Progress of Armour 1914–1918

A Chronology

THE SYMBOL □ DENOTES ACTIVITY OVER A PERIOD OF TIME

1914

AUGUST

1 Germany declares war on Russia, followed on 6th by Austria–Hungary. Germany declares war on France and invades Belgium.

4 Britain declares war on Germany.

12 Start of transportation to France of British Expeditionary Force.

14 French offensive opens in Lorraine.

20 Fall of Brussels.

20–25 Main German force sweeps back Allies at Battles of Mons, the Sambre and the Ardennes.

26–31 Russians crushed at Tannenberg on Germany's Eastern Front.

SEPTEMBER

2 General Kluck's First German Army reaches the Marne 25 miles east of Paris.

5–10 First Battle of the Marne. Germans withdraw to a line Noyon–Verdun.

15–18 First Battle of the Aisne. Armies swing northwards to coast.

OCTOBER–NOVEMBER

□ Heavy fighting in Flanders. BEF denies Channel ports to German Army through First Battle of Ypres (30 October–24 November).

NOVEMBER

1 Allies declare war on Turkey.

DECEMBER

□ Germans dig in along Western Front, establishing static trench warfare from North Sea, near Nieuport, to Swiss border near Belfort.

1915

JANUARY

19–20 First German air raids on England.

JANUARY–JUNE

□ Allied offensives on Western Front beaten back.

FEBRUARY

15 First naval assault at Dardanelles.

18 Opening of first submarine campaign against Allied commerce.

24 British Admiralty Landships Committee set up to examine means of ending trench stalemate.

APRIL

22 First use of gas – by Germans at Second Battle of Ypres.

25 British landings at Gallipoli.

MAY

23 Italy declares war on Austria–Hungary.

JUNE

30 British War Office defines its requirements for an armoured cross-country machine able to cross a trench 10 feet wide.

JUNE–SEPTEMBER

□ Russians retreat to line south of Riga.

SEPTEMBER

22 Successful trials in England of 'Little Willie', first prototype tank.

SEPTEMBER–NOVEMBER

□ Allies renew offensive on Western Front with small success.

DECEMBER

17 General Haig takes over command of BEF.

1916

JANUARY

9 Evacuation completed after unsuccessful Dardanelles Expedition.

29 First official trials of 'Big Willie' or 'Mother', second prototype tank.

FEBRUARY

12 British Tank Supply Committee orders 100 Mark I tanks.

21 First German offensive at Verdun; fighting continues there until December.

MARCH

□ Recruiting begins for 'Heavy Section' of British Machine Gun Corps.

JUNE

24 First Battle of the Somme opens with seven-day artillery assault by Allies; on first day of infantry fighting British suffer 60,000 casualties.

JUNE–SEPTEMBER

□ New Russian offensive under General Brusilov weakens resources of Central Powers, notably at Verdun and in Italy.

JULY

13 British horse cavalry used en masse for last time; mown down by German counter-attack on Somme front.

SEPTEMBER

15 Tanks make first appearance in final phase of Battle of the Somme.

SEPTEMBER–NOVEMBER

□ Tanks make minor sorties at Thiepval, Flers, Le Sars and Beaumont Hamel.

1917

FEBRUARY

1 Germans launch unrestricted submarine warfare against commerce.

FEBRUARY–APRIL

□ Germans withdraw to heavily defended zone – the Hindenburg Line.

MARCH

12 Start of First Russian Revolution.

APRIL

6 USA declares war on Germany.

16 French tanks (artillerie d'assaut) used at Battle of Chemin des Dames.

APRIL–NOVEMBER

□ Tanks, though poorly deployed at Arras, Buillacourt, Messines and Passchendaele, influence morale of both sides.

JUNE

□ First division of American Expeditionary Force shipped to France.

JULY

27 British Tank Corps established by Royal warrant.

OCTOBER–NOVEMBER

□ Italians heavily defeated at Caporetto.

NOVEMBER

7 Second Russian Revolution. Lenin and Trotsky seize power.

20 Mark IV tanks used en masse at Battle of Cambrai to force extensive breach in Hindenburg Line.

DECEMBER

15 Russia and Germany agree armistice terms.

1918

MARCH

21 Ludendorff opens spring offensives on Western Front using Hutier infiltration tactics; first phase ends 5 April.

26 First appearance, at Colincourt, of medium Whippet tanks.

16

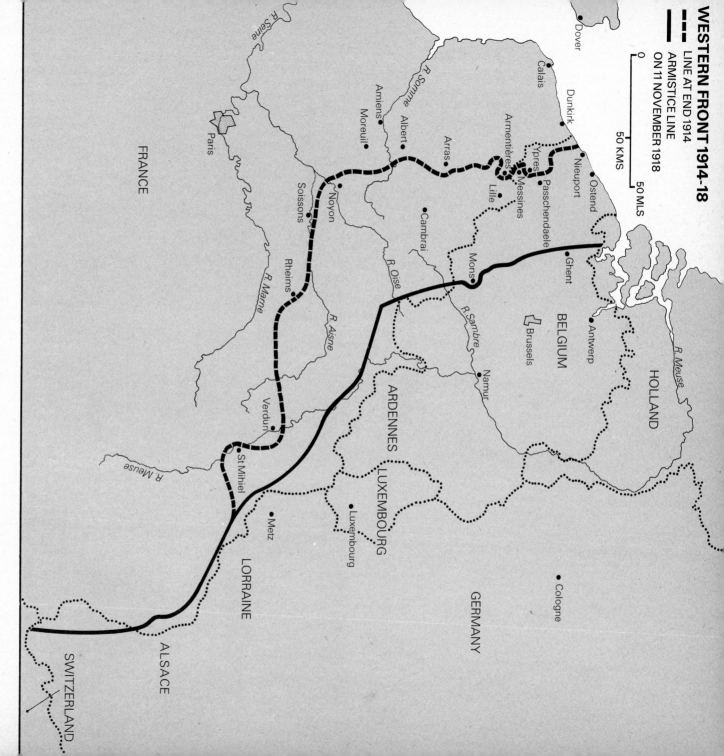

WESTERN FRONT 1914-18

- - - LINE AT END 1914

━━━ ARMISTICE LINE ON 11 NOVEMBER 1918

0   50 KMS

0   50 MLS

FRANCE

SWITZERLAND

ALSACE

LORRAINE

GERMANY

LUXEMBOURG

ARDENNES

BELGIUM

HOLLAND

Dover

Calais

Dunkirk

Ostend

Nieuport

Ypres

Passchendaele

Messines

Armentières

Lille

Albert

Arras

Mons

Ghent

Antwerp

Cologne

Brussels

Namur

Cambrai

Amiens

Moreuil

Paris

Soissons

Noyon

Rheims

Verdun

St Mihiel

Metz

Luxembourg

R. Seine

R. Somme

R. Oise

R. Aisne

R. Marne

R. Sambre

R. Meuse

R. Meuse

APRIL

9-17 Ludendorff's second offensive.

24 First tank v. tank action at Villers-Bretonneux: British Mark IV meets German A7V.

MAY

27 Ludendorff's third offensive begins, reaches the Marne on 30th. US divisions make first major impact in Allied defences. Renault FT light tanks used for first time on 31st.

JUNE–JULY

☐ Further German offensives held.

JULY

4 Mark Vs make successful début spearheading counter-attack at Hamel.

18 Allied counter-offensive begin on Aisne-Marne front.

AUGUST

8 'Black Day' of German Army: 400 heavy and medium Allied tanks advance seven miles in under nine hours at Battle of Amiens.

21 Second phase of Amiens offensive begins.

SEPTEMBER

12-16 American ground and combined ground-air assaults drive Germans out of St Mihiel salient.

26 Americans begin Meuse-Argonne offensive.

27 British begin storming of Hindenburg Line.

28 Allied offensive opens in Flanders.

OCTOBER

6 First German request for armistice.

27 Ludendorff resigns. Austria-Hungary sues for armistice.

29 Mutiny at Kiel of German High Seas Fleet.

31 Revolution in Vienna and Budapest.

NOVEMBER

9 Revolution in Berlin.

10 Flight of Kaiser.

11 Armistice concluded with Germany.

17

Chapter Two
World War I

In this gigantic siege war of the 20th century, a 20th-century solution was needed to break the stalemate that had taken hold in the trenches. When it came it was based, appropriately, upon the device which came to dominate the first half of the century as the queen of inventions – the internal combustion engine, created in 1885 by Gottlieb Daimler and Karl Benz.

Motor vehicles had already appeared on the battlefield: in World War I the lorry and the bus were used to transport men and supplies; and, following the earlier lead of the French firm of Charron-Girardot et Voigt, which in 1904

had developed the first production armoured car, the British Admiralty brought in armoured cars to defend its air squadrons based at Dunkirk. At first the latter were ordinary motor cars fitted with sheets of mild steel boiler plate. Later the firms of Rolls Royce, Wolseley and Lanchester developed custom-built armoured cars, but by the time these machines were ready the opportunities for their use as a new form of mechanized cavalry had been lost – for they were essentially road-bound and could not deploy across the artillery-made bogs that soon appeared along the Western Front.

Artillery tractors, running on caterpillar tracks, were among the few machines able to function normally in the devastated terrain of the Western Front. From them Lt-Col Swinton devised his idea for a new form of armoured vehicle – the tank.

CHARRON ARMOURED CAR 1904

This is what the first production armoured car looked like. It was developed in 1904 by the French firm of Charron-Girardot et Voigt, weighed 3 tons and mounted a fully rotating turret with a machine-gun. On the side of the car channels were provided for crossing ditches.

ROLLS ROYCE ARMOURED CAR 1914

A larger version of the armoured car was the Maxim-armed Rolls Royce model of 1914. Although these were useful behind the lines on the Western Front, they were a failure as mechanized cavalry because they were soon bogged down in the shell-torn landscape. (Elsewhere, in the flat, open spaces of Palestine, they were more successful.)

had found the answer to the problems of the Western Front, he presented his ideas in a paper to GHQ in France; there it received a brutal rebuff from generals who were not only ignorant of modern technology but were also totally committed to the gospel which proclaimed the sanctity of personal combat. Swinton sent a copy of his paper to his good friend and mentor, Lt-Col Maurice Hankey, at that time Secretary to the Committee of Imperial Defence in London. Hankey was impressed with Swinton's ideas, reproduced them in the form of a Cabinet Memorandum and tried at the same time to lobby support in Whitehall. In this period of the war all questions connected with British fighting motor vehicles were regarded as the province of the Royal Navy, and so Hankey's memorandum was circulated through the various channels of the Admiralty.

In January 1915 the paper reached the desk of Winston Churchill, then First Lord of the Admiralty; he, suitably impressed with the idea, enlisted the support of the Prime Minister, Lord Asquith. Two Holt tractors were evaluated by a small select body of experts, which in turn reported favourably, and Churchill created the Admiralty Landships Committee to examine the concept in greater depth and detail. One lasting result, incidentally, of the Admiralty's involvement in these early stages is that certain naval terms then came into use which persisted, various parts of the tank being referred to as the hull, turret, deck, sponson, barbette, superstructure, bow, etc.

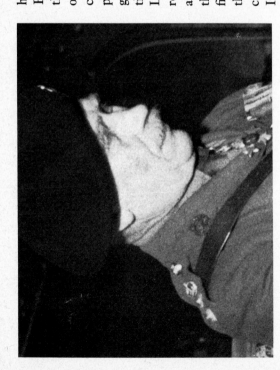

One of the official British war correspondents, or 'Eye witnesses', as they were called, was Lt-Col Ernest Swinton. In October 1914 he had seen an American invention, the Holt caterpillar tractor, being used to pull heavy artillery behind the lines. He was struck with the idea of arming and armouring these vehicles as an antidote to the barbed wire and the machine-guns of the Germans. Swinton was an engineer by profession, and he had also written the official British military history of the Russo-Japanese War in Manchuria, which in 1904 had produced the first war of trench stalemate in the 20th century. Convinced that he

brain-child and bombarded GHQ with papers on how the new weapon might be used. A final field demonstration was held in England, to which Haig, the British commander, undoubtedly prompted by Churchill, sent an engineering officer on his staff, Major Hugh Elles, as official observer. The final demonstration was a great success and Lloyd George ordered his ministry to put the tank into quantity production.

The first British model, designated the Mark I (of which 150 were to be built) was produced in two types: a 'male', weighing 31 tons and mounting two 6-pounder naval cannon and four machine-guns; and a 'female', weighing 30 tons and armed with six machine-guns. At a maximum speed of 3.7 mph these tanks, fitted with wrap-round tracks which completely embraced the hull, could traverse obstacles 4½ feet high and negotiate a trench 11½ feet wide. They were remarkable machines but suffered from a host of teething troubles and their first designers felt that they needed more time before the tanks could be considered ready for combat. But they were denied this luxury for, in the later summer of 1916, Haig and his armies found themselves in a desperate plight. In order to draw German pressure away from the French at Verdun he had been forced prematurely to commit the new and raw divisions of Kitchener's army to an offensive along the Somme Valley. The first phase of the great offensive had stalled on the wire of the German trenches and Haig next called for tanks to be committed to the battle at the earliest opportunity.

The first tanks did not leave the factories in England until July and it was August before 50 tanks could be shipped out to France. A new organization had been created to man and fight the tanks which, for security purposes, was called the 'heavy' section of the Machine Gun Corps. The initial establishment was 184 officers and 1,600 men and their tanks were divided into six companies of four sections; there were three 'male' and three 'female' tanks to each section.

The main defect of the Mark I tank – besides its mechanical unreliability – was the tremendous strain it placed on the eight-man crew. The noise inside the hull was so great that conversation was impossible and the driver had to communicate his orders to the gearsman by banging a hammer on the engine cover to a set code. It was impossible to stand upright in the tank and the temperature inside after some 30 minutes rose to well over 100°F. In action crews drank up to a gallon of water per day per man. After some hours they would emerge sick and often mildy delirious from the hot fume-filled hulls. Very few of these tank men had seen action on the Western Front and they were drawn from all branches of the arms and services. Nevertheless the demands of strategy dictated that inexperienced men, who hardly had had enough time to get to know one another or their machines, were committed to battle in tanks which themselves had not been tested under battle conditions.

Meanwhile Swinton, now back in France, but shortly to return to London, made one more attempt to interest the High Command in his idea for an armoured fighting vehicle. He submitted a new paper entitled *The Armoured Machine Gun Destroyer* and this time he received a more sympathetic response from GHQ; they passed it on to the War Office to examine new ideas. In June 1915 Swinton was back in London (as Secretary to the Dardanelles Committee) and there he learned for the first time of the progress of the Admiralty Landships Committee. An engineering company called Fosters, of Lincoln, which built heavy artillery tractors, had by this time produced a prototype vehicle. This was in due course commonly called 'Little Willie'.

However, the Admiralty Committee was by now in deep trouble; it had run foul of the new Ministry of Munitions under Lloyd George, who felt that it was poaching in the Ministry's domain, and dissension was rife. The Prime Minister next ordered the two factions to combine, and a new organization was set up entitled the Experiments Committee, in which the original Admiralty personnel apparently retained a controlling interest. In September 1915 a design team consisting of Fosters, William Tritton and Lt W. G. Wilson overcame certain problems with the tracks which had beset the original prototype and a new machine, known as 'Big Willie', was built. It was at this point that the word 'tank' was coined by Swinton. For reasons of security, the hull and chassis for the experimental vehicle had been constructed in different shops and the hull had been referred to as a water-carrier or water-tank, for use in Mesopotamia. Swinton later recalled this in the autumn of 1915 when everyone concerned was trying to think of a name for the new vehicle; he suggested the adoption of the word 'tank', which has since come into use in almost every language in the world.

After the failure of the Dardanelles Expedition Churchill, as its creator, was ousted from the Cabinet and in a fit of pique returned to his first profession, soldiering, and soon found himself as second-in-command of a Guards battalion on the Western Front. He still regarded the tank as his

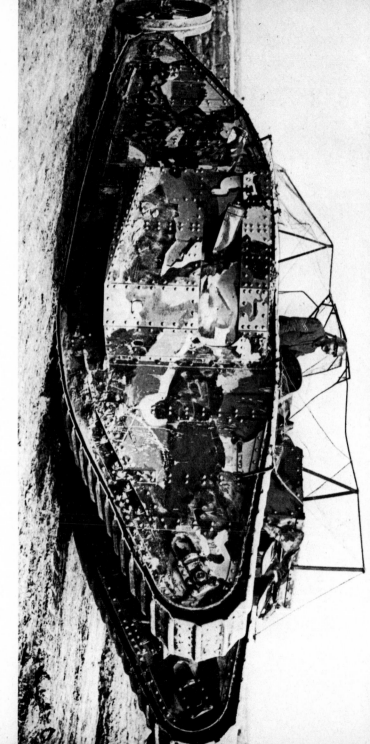

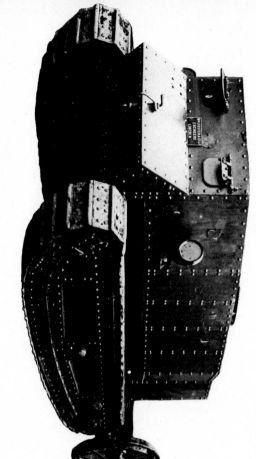

OPPOSITE The Killen Strait tractor, an experimental tracked vehicle fitted with a 'torpedo' wire-cutter.
THIS PAGE The first British tank to appear was 'Little Willie' (left). Next came 'Big Willie' or 'Mother' (top); the rear wheels acted as a steering 'tail'. From this design the first Mark 1 tanks were produced. 'Male' versions had 6-pounder guns in the sponsons, while the 'female' version (centre) carried machine-guns clad in armoured jackets. Note also the anti-grenade netting on the 'female'.

23

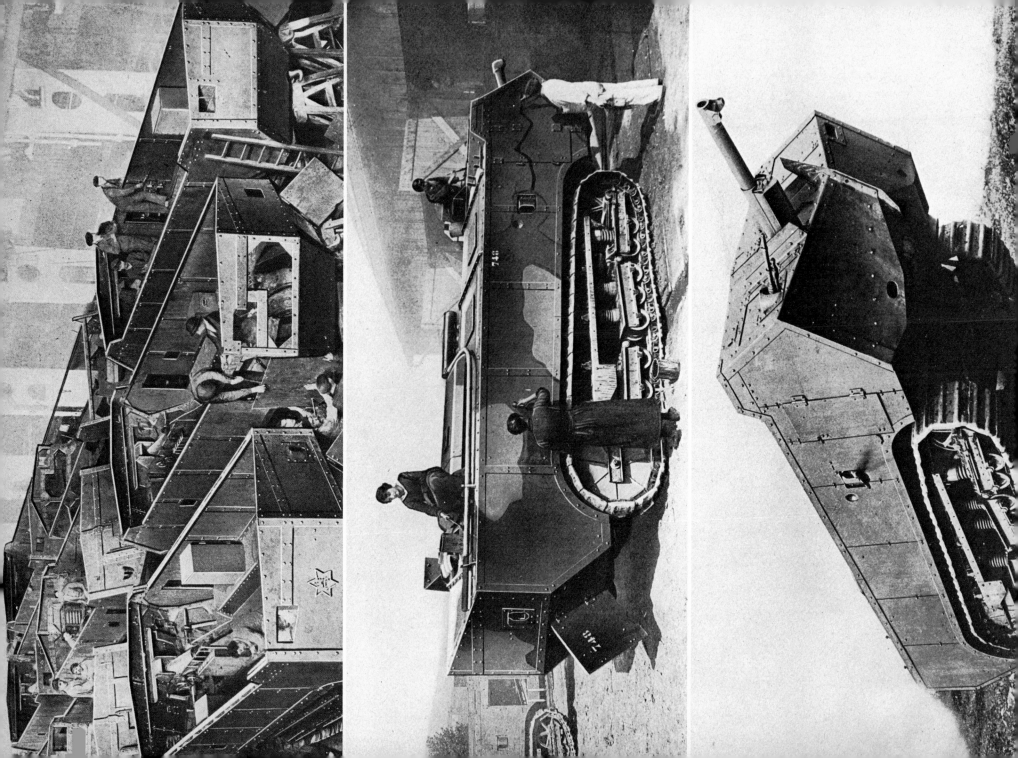

The generals were only too well aware of the folly of going against the time-honoured principle that a brand new weapon, particularly one like the tank which represented a revolutionary design in warfare, needs a small battlefield trial; but to have done so would have destroyed the all-important advantage of surprise.

On 15 September 1916, 49 tanks rumbled towards their start-lines to spearhead the assault by Rawlinson's Fourth Army in the final phase of the Battle of the Somme. Even then surprise, in the strategic sense, was lacking, since Rawlinson heralded the advance by a pre-battle bombardment of 1,250 guns (one gun for every three yards of front) which lasted three days. Only 36 tanks then crossed the start-lines and many more were quickly disabled in the cauldron of no man's land. Nevertheless, where the tanks, either alone or in groups, broke through the German defences their impact was immediate and a new dimension in terror warfare had been created.

Few tanks were in any fit condition to engage in combat after the first day but Haig and many of his commanders felt that the new weapon system had earned a second and bigger chance. He requested that 1,000 tanks be produced for the following year and on 8 October 1916 supported the establishment of a separate Tank Corps. Elles, who had been with the tanks from the beginning, was confirmed as commander of the new organization, and as his chief staff officer he was given the brilliant if temperamental Major J. F. C. Fuller, a man who brought genuinely original ideas to the tactical side of tank warfare. Together Elles and Fuller formed a unique and successful partnership which created out of an amorphous collection of men and machines a coherent fighting force. Volunteers flocked to join the new corps, men of skill and enthusiasm many of whom had experienced combat as soldiers on the Western Front and who therefore readily understood the vital role that tanks

could play. The tanks, also, were new: there had been a considerable improvement in tank technology and design, and in the spring of 1917 the Mark IV appeared in France, a better armoured and mechanically more reliable tank than the Mark I had been on its début.

BRITISH MARK IV (MALE) TANK 1917

The Mark IV was the first tank to be used en masse and was the key vehicle at Cambrai (see also pages 30–31). It kept the rhomboidal shape of its predecessors but had thicker armour (up to 12 mm), a shorter and handier 6-pounder gun, and was the first to carry the excellent Lewis machine-gun.

The front view (left) shows the observation ports for the driver and the commander, the 6-pounder and Lewis gun mounted in each side sponson, the unditching beam chained on top, and the extended track 'grousers', which improved the vehicle's running performance over difficult terrain.

The 28-ton 'male' was 26 feet 5 inches long, 12 feet 9 inches wide and 8 feet 2 inches high. It had a trench-crossing capacity of 10 feet and a maximum speed of 3.7 mph. Its crew of 8 was armed with two 6-pounder (57-mm) guns and four Lewis machine-guns.

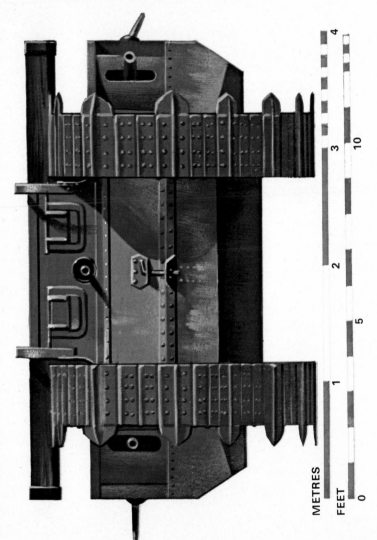

METRES

FEET

The side view (below) shows the cylindrical exhaust silencer on top of the tank; behind it are the manhole turret, and, beneath the unditching beam, the box for the towing rope. To the rear of the ball-mounted Lewis gun is the right sponson door. The crewman wears a leather helmet and face visor to guard against 'splash' – the metal splinters which after a hit flew about the vehicle's interior.

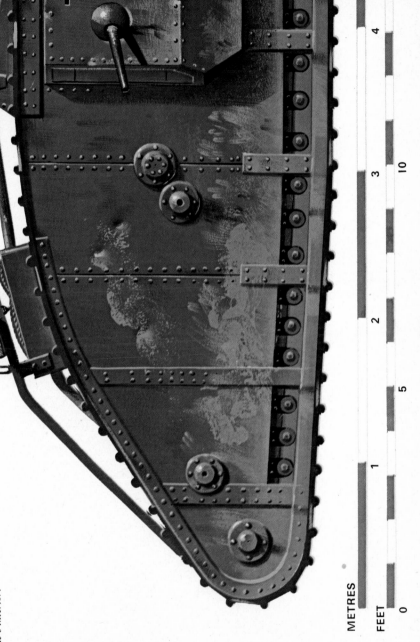

METRES

FEET

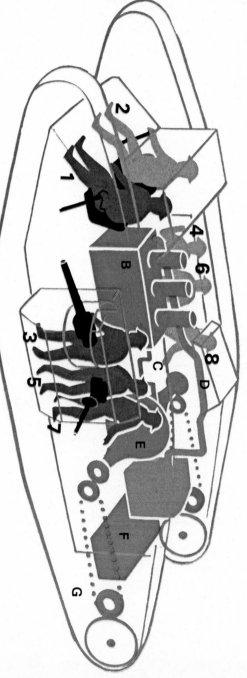

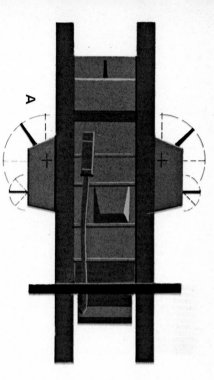

These diagrams show the positions of the chief working parts and the cramped conditions — especially in the sponsons — in which the crews had to operate. Each crew consisted of: 1 Commander (also brakeman and machine-gunner); 2 Driver; 3, 4 Principal gunners; 5, 6 Machine-gunners; 7, 8 Gearsmen (one for each track).

A Arcs of fire
B Petrol engine
C Starting handle
D Tubular radiator
E Transmission (worm reduction gear)
F Fuel tank
G Track driving chain

Tank crews were equipped with special overalls, gauntlets and reinforced leather helmets. On each side of the turret was an episcope and a pistol port for close-range action. The side view also shows the armoured hood fitted to the hull machine-gun.

5   6   7   8

20   25

LEFT *Col J. E. Estienne, leader of the pro-armour school in France.*

OPPOSITE *The British gun-carrier tank (above), whose potential as offensive mobile artillery was never realized; it mounted a 60-pounder gun, the wheels being removed and chained to the hull sides. Below are French Renault FT tanks; these versions are armed with the short cannon.*

with their tank than the British but would not be rushed into premature employment in battle, and it was not until April 1917 and the Battle of Chemin des Dames that the French tank received its baptism of fire.

It was still later – November 1917 and the Battle of Cambrai – before Elles and Fuller were allowed to deploy tanks en masse and in tune with the tactical doctrine which they had evolved. The Allied situation by this time was grave: the French armies were recovering from wide-scale mutinies, the Italians had suffered a major reverse at Caporetto and the Russian Front in the East had collapsed. Politically the Allied cause was in desperate need of a victory; the only bright star on the horizon was the entry of the United States into the war (in April 1917) but at that time all she had to offer was a vast reserve of untrained manpower.

Originally Fuller had conceived Cambrai as a tank raid in a sector where the terrain had not been ploughed into a bog by the artillery. The Allied search for a military victory of major dimensions, fortified by the enthusiasm of General Byng and the Third Army, transformed the operation into one in which the tanks would aim to secure a rupture of the German front through which the Cavalry Corps – with 40,000 horsemen – could exploit and perhaps lead the way to a crushing victory. It is the paradox of Cambrai that while in many ways it was one of the most ineptly conceived battles in British military history, it also contained, at least in the plan for the initial assault, a daring, meticulously thought-out and superbly executed tactical experiment which changed the nature of war.

The initial problem was that of breaching the formidable defences of the Hindenburg Line, which had three lines of mutually supporting trenches, ample artillery fire support and avenues of barbed wire. The operational plan devised by Fuller was accepted by all but one of the assault divisions (the 51st Highlanders). There was to be no long pre-battle bombardment, which had so often in the past robbed offensives of any strategic surprise. The artillery instead was to open fire with a hurricane bombardment as the tanks moved forward, and aircraft were to be used to supplement the guns by strafing the forward gun positions and the German lines of communications. The tanks operated in groups of three and each tank carried a fascine weighing 1¼ tons which it dropped in the trench; four platoons of infantry advancing in close column (rather than the traditional method of extended line) moved forward in support of each group of tanks.

At first tanks were used in driblets and with little effect. In 1917, at the Battles of Arras, Buillacourt, Messines and Passchendaele, the tanks were wastefully deployed in pairs behind the usual artillery bombardment. But despite their misuse the presence of the tanks raised Allied and lowered German morale. The German High Command, for its part, had completely dismissed the tank as a viable weapon system. The Germans saw it primarily as a terror weapon, which could be countered by the high morale of their own troops and the skill of specially trained artillery batteries. (There were a number of Holt tractors in Germany and the Army did develop a wooden mock-up on a chassis but at this stage did not proceed any further.)

The French, led in this respect by Colonel J. E. Estienne, were if anything even more enthusiastic than the British – although their development of the tank proceeded along entirely different lines; there is, moreover, no evidence of any collusion between the two Allies. By the spring of 1916 the French companies of St Chamond and Schneider had developed what were really two versions of an assault gun: they were called *artillerie d'assaut* and were in effect nothing more than the excellent French 75-mm cannon mounted forward on a Holt chassis and enclosed in an armoured box. The French had more teething troubles

28

THE TANKS AT CAMBRAI

The Allied plan of attack used tanks in groups of three to bridge the German trenches of the Hindenburg Line. The Mark IVs leading the assault carried fascines which they dropped in the trenches in the sequence shown in the diagram. Behind the armour came the infantry, now moving in close column rather than in the traditional method of extended line; the assault groups were started about 300 yards apart. These tactics produced, by the end of the first day, a major breach in the German defences some six miles wide and 4,000 yards deep. Back in England church bells hailed a great victory; but failure to exploit the advance produced in turn a German counter-attack which ten days later straightened the salient.

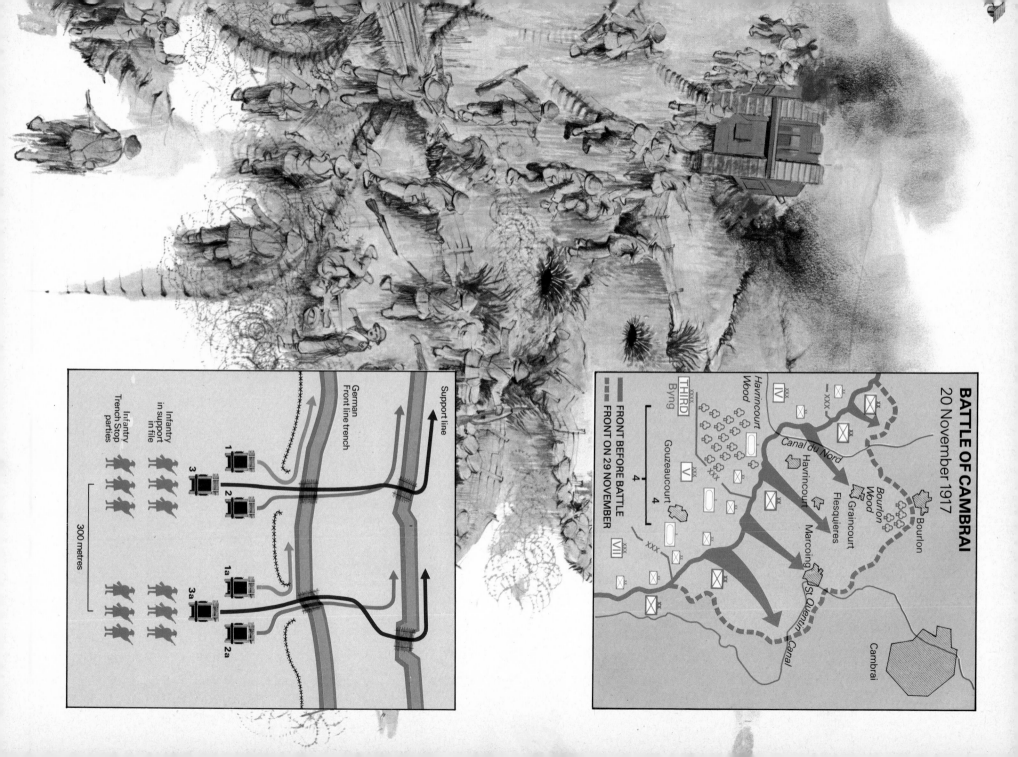

Left inset diagram

Support line

German Front line trench

300 metres

Infantry
Trench Stop
parties

Infantry
in support
in file

1

3

2

1a

3a

2a

Right inset diagram

BATTLE OF CAMBRAI
20 November 1917

FRONT BEFORE BATTLE

FRONT ON 29 NOVEMBER

THIRD
Byng

Havrincourt
Wood

IV

V

VII

Gouzeaucourt

Canal du Nord

Havrincourt

Bourlon
Wood

Bourlon

Flesquières

Graincourt

Marcoing

St. Quentin
Canal

Cambrai

4

4

Everyone was reasonably optimistic about the plans for the advance and breakthrough of the German front; there were doubts, however, about the plans for the exploitation phase. Haig's chief intelligence officer, Brigadier-General John Charteris, succinctly summed up the situation when he wrote in his diary: 'We shall be alright at first, afterwards is in the lap of the God of Battle'. This was so because there were no reserves either of infantry or tanks available to exploit success, and everything depended upon the performance of the four divisions of cavalry in both the timing of their move through the ruptured front and in their ability to exploit the ground beyond.

Except for the comparative failure of the 51st Highland Division, everything went according to plan on 20 November 1917. A solid phalanx of 476 tanks crawled forward across no man's land and penetrated the bloody chaos caused by the initial artillery bombardment. Behind the fighting tanks and their jubilant infantry moved a new phenomenon on the battlefield, a mechanized army of radio tanks, wire-pulling tanks and supply tanks ready to support the spearhead formations.

By the end of the first day, and at a cost of fewer than 4,000 casualties, a breach six miles wide and 4,000 yards deep had been achieved; the church bells pealed out the news of a victory in England that night. If the battle had been terminated at that point and kept within Fuller's original concept of a tank raid then indeed it would have been a great victory. But the commanders demanded exploitation. The cavalry had already failed once to break through and so the infantry and a few surviving tanks[1] were ordered to widen the breach and make it yet more

secure for the horsemen. Resilient German defences blocked the advance and the last British reserves were exchanged for extra ground that was measured in yards. Ludendorff, the German commander, counter-attacked the salient on 30 November and in places the British fell back to beyond their original start-line. But at least the tanks were not blamed for the subsequent disasters, and indeed at Gouzeaucourt they gained fresh laurels when the German advance was reversed by a timely tank counter-attack – which to some extent proved that tanks could hold as well as capture ground.

The battle of Cambrai was the first major demonstration of tank power. It showed that tanks, operating en masse but with surprise and on firm ground could, when adequately supported by infantry and artillery, achieve rapid and complete command over the strongest dug-in defences. But there remained the unresolved problem of exploitation. Some writers have criticized Fuller and Elles for not keeping back more tanks to ensure an adequate reserve for the days following the initial attack. But such criticisms lack validity because if fewer tanks had been used on the first day the dimensions of the rupture would have been that much smaller, so leaving the reserves an even greater task. In any case the Mark IV, though an excellent tank, was not suited to the role of exploitation; it was slow, too heavy, and it lacked the necessary endurance. Since horse cavalry had proved even more unsuited to the task there grew up a demand for a lighter, faster tank which could meet the needs and rigours of exploitation. The French had already developed such a vehicle in the excellent Renault FT, the first tank to be built with a revolving turret, but there is no evidence to suggest that the British were interested in either acquiring or copying it for their own needs.

---

[1] Only 100 tanks were fit for combat duty after the first day at Cambrai.

32

OPPOSITE AND BELOW *The photograph opposite well illustrates the roles in which early tanks were most effective, i.e. as obstacle-crossing, wire-crushing weapons of terror. Faced by such monsters, which its own General Staff was reluctant to copy, the German propaganda machine struck back with encouraging material (below) showing how vulnerable tanks were to the Kaiser's flamethrowers. RIGHT A British observation post at Cambrai, stationed on a broken-down Mark IV tank. (The initials WC stand for Wire Cutter.)*

By the spring of 1918 ever-increasing numbers of the United States Army had arrived in France. At first the Americans had expressed little interest in the tank: although they had a number of prototypes under development there was little urgency to build a battle tank for the Army. However, Cambrai completely changed American thinking. The US Army began to demand its own tanks but then found that American industry could not produce anything suitable in time; consequently the newly formed American tank corps was equipped with British and French tanks.

In the meantime the German Army, not surprisingly, was also feeling the strain and pressure of almost four years of incessant warfare. Her associates were faltering and the

Allied naval blockade of her ports was causing widespread deprivation to the German population. Submarine warfare had failed either to starve Britain into submission or to halt the arrival of American troops. Ludendorff, gathering together the last of his reserves, planned to launch a major offensive against the British (whom he considered the most vulnerable of the Allies) and thereby win peace. Tanks were not to figure in any real scale in this offensive, there being only a handful of clumsy 30-ton land fortresses available (called the A7V). The Germans were to rely for their mobility on new tactics which had been devised for the infantry — from which the concept of Blitzkrieg, or lightning war, was eventually to evolve. These were infiltration tactics, sometimes known as Hutier tactics after the German general who

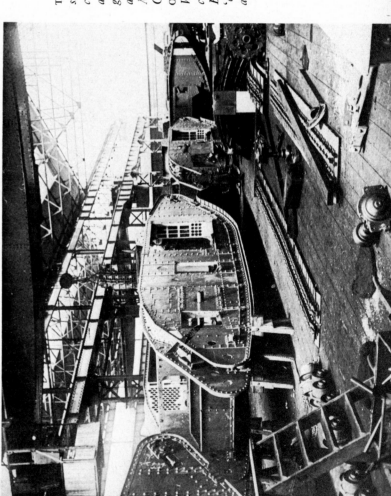

had first used them (on the Eastern Front at Riga in 1917). The tactics introduced a new type of infantryman, the 'stormtrooper': armed with the newly developed Bergmann submachine-gun, he moved at speed through the enemy's lines, bypassing strongpoints which were dealt with by the main body of the infantry following on behind.

In March 1918 Allied armies reeled back under the shock of the first German hammer-blows. Such tanks as were deployed in the defence were used in penny packets as mobile pillboxes. These posed little problem to the Germans but elsewhere tanks came together in fighting groups and made a major contribution to stemming the momentum of the German advance. Behind the front line the Allied commanders carefully husbanded resources and pre-

pared for the moment when the German advance lost its main thrust and they could counter-attack. Two new tanks had been built by the British, the medium 'Whippet' and the Mark V, the latter being a major improvement on earlier models since it required only one man to drive the tank – instead of as many as four, as had been the case with Marks I–IV. At Hamel, 60 Mark Vs led a counter-attack by the Australians under General Monash (who also had some American infantry companies in the operation) and inflicted a resounding defeat on the Germans. This operation saw the most decisive use of tanks to date, success being achieved through the precise co-ordination of infantry and tanks in the assault.

In July 1918 it became obvious that the German advance

Numbers of Fighting Tanks
WORLD WAR 1

CATEGORY	BRITAIN	FRANCE	GERMANY
Heavy tanks	1,970	—	20
Medium (Whippet) and artillerie d'assaut (St Chamond, Schneider)	240	800	—
Light tanks (Renault FT)	—	3,500	—

had been held, and as the troops consolidated along the new defence perimeter the three Allied leaders, Foch (who now was commander-in-chief of all Allied forces), Haig and General John J. Pershing of the American Expeditionary Force, met to plan the counter-blows. German morale was on the point of collapse and this the Allied commanders intended to exploit in a series of strong, carefully spaced offensives: the French were to attack along the Aisne and Marne, the British at Amiens and the American Corps in the St Mihiel salient south of Verdun. At Amiens Rawlinson, now a convert to armour, followed the precedent set by Monash and deployed the smallest practicable force of infantry with the largest practicable force of tanks. On the morning of 8 August 1918, 400 Allied tanks spearheaded the assault of eight divisions of infantry. The Germans were

caught completely by surprise and a major rupture of their front occurred. By early afternoon the third Allied objective was taken (see map), which also meant that Rawlinson's Fourth Army had advanced more than seven miles in less than nine hours. For exploitation the British had massed a mixed force of Medium A Whippets, horse cavalry and armoured cars. The cavalry and tanks failed to achieve any meaningful co-operation but the armoured cars, towed by heavy tanks across the front and then 'unleashed' beyond the third line, caused havoc among the retreating and disorganized Germans. After 10 August the battle lost much of its momentum, most of the tanks had become casualties[2] and the infantry, by now so heavily dependent on tanks, would not advance without their support.

2 145 tanks were available on 9 August, 63 on the 10th and 38 on the 11th.

LEFT *A captured British tank at Armentières, re-painted in German markings.*

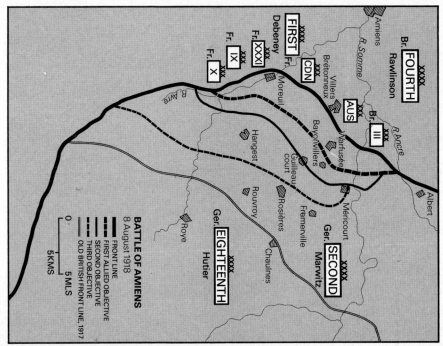

BATTLE OF AMIENS
8 August 1918

FRONT LINE
FIRST ALLIED OBJECTIVE
SECOND OBJECTIVE
THIRD OBJECTIVE
OLD BRITISH FRONT LINE, 1917

0   5KMS
0   5MLS

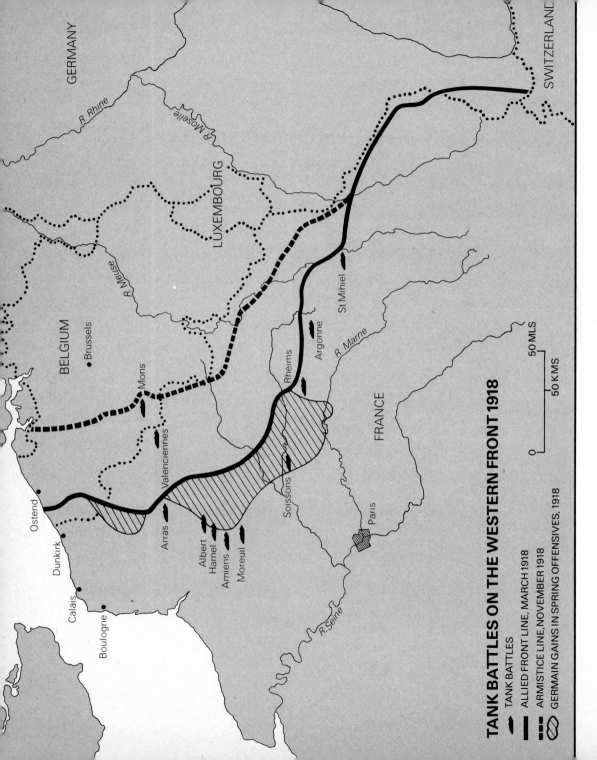

In the event the Germans credited the British with a victory and for that reason 8 August is referred to as the 'Black Day' in the annals of the German Army. Ludendorff believed that the Germans lost the war on that day; morale was irretrievably broken and although he was still able to stabilize the front and contain Allied advances, the heart had gone out of his soldiers and staff officers alike. Very few Germans were in fact killed by tank fire: its lurching hull, poor field of fire and restricted vision did not make for a stable gun platform; but as a morale-breaker it was superb.

Throughout August and September Foch launched major offensives along the whole front and the tanks played their part in maintaining the momentum of the Allied advance. The final phase of the war saw the German Army trading space for time in front of the British, using river and canal lines and holding doggedly to the rugged terrain of the Argonne against the Americans.

In the early autumn the Americans, in a series of brilliant offensives spearheaded by tanks, cleared the Argonne while the British broke out into the more open country beyond Le Cateau. The Germans fell back skilfully and never really lost their cohesion, and in this way they were undoubtedly aided by the comparative ineffectiveness at this stage of the Allied tanks. Now these mechanically unreliable machines had to operate ever farther from their base repair shops, and they broke down more and more frequently. The cavalry could do little since it was still compromised by the machine-gun and by rearguard German artillery. Nevertheless tactical improvisation with the tank abounded during the closing stages of the war. Night attacks were attempted and co-operation with aircraft, which had already played a major part in the success of previous operations, reached new heights. A number of tank-versus-tank encounters occurred right up to the last days of the war and, ominously enough, the British Tank Corps began to acknowledge that the Germans, despite their still more limited experience, were proving to be very effective in their handling of the new vehicles.

ABOVE *American-manned tanks in action on the Western Front in 1918. After Cambrai the US Army was keen to acquire its own armoured fighting vehicles, but American industry was not in a position to produce them in time.*

BELOW *From necessity the Americans relied on Allied tanks such as these and French Renault FT 17s.*

39

Chapter Three

The Inter-War Years

weapon systems would have been resolved. Instead these issues were destined to provide the forum for debate, speculation and eventually bitter controversy in the inter-war period.

France had ended the war with the largest army and the biggest stockpile of tanks and she now led the field in tank tactics and deployment. However, the little Renault FT, which provided the bulk of France's 3,000 tanks, was suited only to an infantry-supporting role. In due course this great quantity of light tanks, coupled with problems of economic retrenchment, meant that French armoured doctrine was held back for more than a decade; the Renault FT, though an efficient tank in itself, became in effect a millstone to further progress.

In Britain Fuller launched the first salvo in the great debate with Plan 1919; thereafter he acted as the driving force in the tank lobby while the Royal Tank Corps (constituted in 1923 as a permanent body with four battalions) provided the battleground over which the arguments raged. In the beginning the military hierarchy gave little support to Fuller and his ideas on the strategic role of armour. The prevailing attitude towards peace, added to conditions of economic strain and the traumatic influence of the Great War, were factors hardly conducive to the promulgation of new doctrines. In 1924 the Tank Corps received its first post-war tank, the Vickers Medium Mark I. Armed with a cannon and a machine-gun in a fully revolving turret and with respectable endurance capabilities, it was the first tank which was able to translate Fuller's theories into practice.

These new plans for armoured warfare had begun to attract a lot of attention and one of the first to support them was Basil Liddell-Hart, a one-time career officer who in 1924 was forced into early retirement because of ill health.

In many of its later aspects World War I had evolved as a tank war – even though the cease-fire came before the true potential of the tank could be properly demonstrated. Had Fuller, for instance, been able to implement his famous Plan 1919 (see diagram) then Western Europe would have witnessed the deployment of tanks and aircraft on an unprecedented scale, and many of the questions left unanswered concerning the strategic potential of these new

ABOVE *Colonel, later Major-General, J. F. C. Fuller, who at the close of the war led British thinking in the use of armour.* OPPOSITE *Fuller's Plan 1919 (above) with which he planned to crush the enemy had the war continued for a fifth year; and (below) the Medium D tank that he envisaged as a spearhead but which in the event never went into production.*

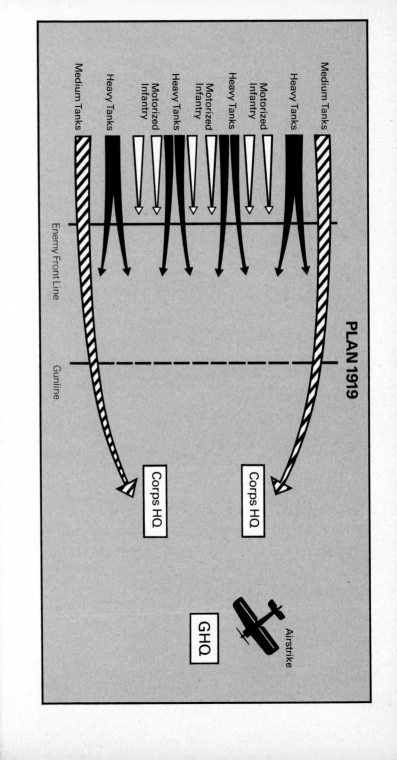

PLAN 1919

Medium Tanks

Heavy Tanks

Motorized Infantry

Motorized Infantry

Heavy Tanks

Motorized Infantry

Heavy Tanks

Motorized Infantry

Motorized Infantry

Heavy Tanks

Medium Tanks

Enemy Front Line

Gunline

Corps HQ

Corps HQ

Airstrike

GHQ

THE EXPERIMENTAL MECHANIZED FORCE 1927

The Force, assembled for demonstrations on Salisbury Plain, England, incorporated all the units of the different arms that had been mechanized by that date and were available for inclusion. It contained every important element of armoured formations of the future – with the exception of specialized vehicles for crossing gaps and clearing minefields. Although at little more than brigade strength, the Force was entirely self-sufficient, even to the extent of having its own RAF air support squadrons. Its composition is shown below:

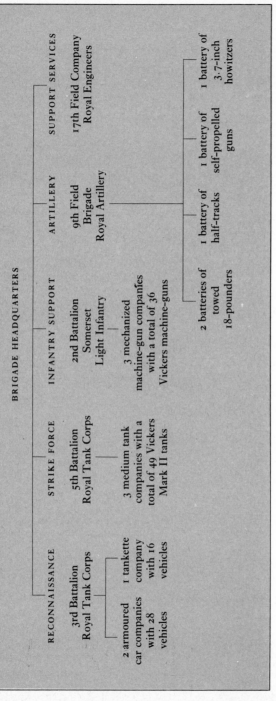

BRIGADE HEADQUARTERS

RECONNAISSANCE

3rd Battalion Royal Tank Corps

2 armoured car companies with 28 vehicles

1 tankette company with 16 vehicles

STRIKE FORCE

5th Battalion Royal Tank Corps

3 medium tank companies with a total of 49 Vickers Mark II tanks

INFANTRY SUPPORT

2nd Battalion Somerset Light Infantry

3 mechanized machine-gun companies with a total of 36 Vickers machine-guns

ARTILLERY

9th Field Brigade Royal Artillery

2 batteries of towed 18-pounders

1 battery of half-tracks

1 battery of self-propelled guns

SUPPORT SERVICES

17th Field Company Royal Engineers

1 battery of 3.7-inch howitzers

In 1920 Liddell-Hart had rewritten the official infantry manuals in the light of the tactics used by the Germans in the spring offensive of 1918. After studying Fuller's ideas he became convinced for an independent role for the tank that the new infantry manuals were in fact better suited to the tank. In 1925 Liddell-Hart was appointed Military Correspondent of the London *Daily Telegraph*, and with Fuller's influence by that time on the wane he used this medium to continue the battle against an ambivalent General Staff. He also made profitable use of his many contacts within the War Office and generally acted as a pamphleteer, disseminating the ideas of others through his newspaper articles, and later through his books. He differed from Fuller in that he was far more involved in expounding the strategic potential of the tank, and unfortunately many of the tactical problems in his doctrine were often glossed over. Nevertheless this doctrine took shape and substance as the concept of the 'Indirect Approach', in which he evolved a method of attack which was designed to turn 'opportunism into a system'.

Liddell-Hart envisaged a moving torrent of tanks which would attack a fortified front along the line of least expectation, sapping, crumbling and eventually overwhelming strongpoints before pouring through to achieve strategic exploitation behind the enemy's lines. The object was to paralyse the 'brain' or central nervous system of the opposing forces (headquarters, supply dumps, etc.); this, Liddell-Hart thought, could be achieved through the persistent pace and momentum of the advance. He saw infantry and

artillery as providing support to the armour; when suitably mounted in their own vehicles the former would also be able to keep in touch with the advance. Additional artillery was to come from tactical air forces capable of providing instant and telling fire support to an army on the move.

The imaginative and highly persuasive writings of both Liddell-Hart and Fuller within a few years attracted new disciples to the 'cause', among them men of high calibre and vision like Hobart, Lindsay and Broad. But against this rising tide of reform was ranged the full weight of the stolid military hierarchy. This powerful body, although reluctant to concede ground, eventually in 1927 sanctioned the creation of an 'experimental brigade' to test the new theories (see diagram). Demonstrations were held on Salisbury Plain and witnessed by official observers from the United States and Europe; these proved an obvious success and the overseas observers returned home suitably impressed. However, the ravages of unemployment and the frightening financial disasters occurring all over the world prevented the much-needed reformation in the doctrine and deployment of tanks from being fully implemented. In 1929 Colonel Broad completed his official report on British tank experiments and the pamphlet, entitled *Mechanized and Armoured Formations*, was given a restricted circulation. But its contents leaked to the Press and, more ominously, were reproduced in their entirety in Germany, where they came into the hands of that country's leading exponent of tank warfare, Colonel Heinz Guderian.

RIGHT Captain Basil Liddell Hart, whose influential writings on the strategic potential of the tank centred round its use in armoured torrents, forcing a substantial breach in the enemy's lines and then assaulting and paralysing his 'brain', i.e. his headquarters and central supply systems.

BELOW Vickers Mark II medium tanks emerge from a smoke screen during the manœuvres of the Experimental Mechanized Force, 1927.

ABOVE *The Italians produced several design advances in the Fiat 2000 (1918) which had a fully rotating turret armed with a 65-mm cannon and thick, 20-mm armour with which to resist the growing firepower envisaged in future wars.*

BELOW *The Fiat 3000 (1920) was a more modest concept based on the Renault FT; 100 were built.*

The German Army of the Weimar Republic was restricted to 100,000 men and was denied the use of tanks, aircraft and heavy artillery under the Treaty of Versailles, signed in June 1919. This gave the Germans a small but distinct advantage in that they were not saddled with a great deal of obsolete equipment, as was the case with their former enemies. But the terms of the treaty also meant that any interest the Germans showed in new weapons had to be taken in a clandestine manner. The dire impact on morale of events in 1918 had provided a lesson which the new German Army, a small but élite force, was determined to benefit from, and in the early 1920s the Army set about acquiring its own tanks. In Sweden the Bofors Company built small quantities of a German tank, the LK II, under licence; but greater progress was made as a result of a secret agreement made with the Soviet Union. This marriage of mutual advantage resulted in the establishment of a tank school in Kazan, deep inside the Tartar Republic and beyond the scrutiny of the complacent Western powers. At first the Swedish-built tank was shipped into Russia and assembled at Kazan but in 1930 the Russians purchased the British Carden Loyd light tank from which was developed the Pzkw I (Panzerkampfwagen I).

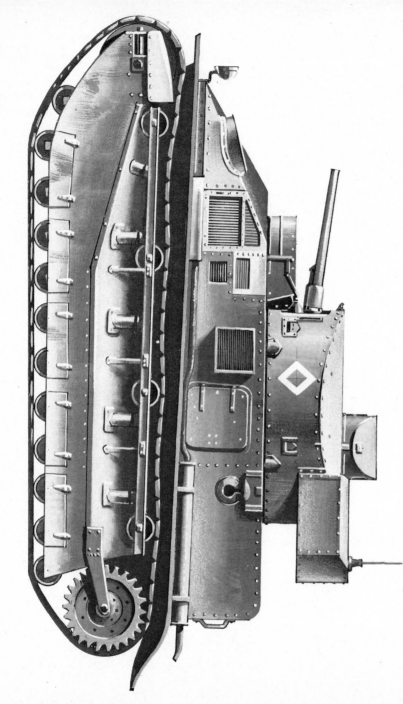

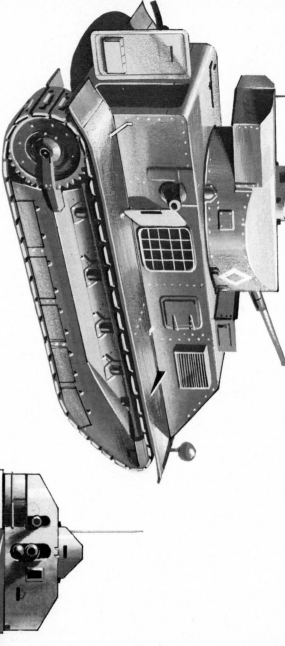

VICKERS MEDIUM 1927

Production of the Vickers Medium tank began in 1923, and some 160 Marks I and II were built. In shape the Vickers Medium stands between the lozenge of World War I and the low profile of the modern battle tank. It was the first tank in the British Army to have all-round traverse and geared elevation for the gun.

The Medium Mark II shown here weighed 12·5 tons; it was 17 feet 6 inches long (overall), 9 feet 2 inches wide and 9 feet 3 inches high. Armour was thin (8 mm) and the main armament, a 3-pounder (47-mm) gun, was unable to fire a satisfactory high-explosive shell; secondary fire came from four Hotchkiss machine-guns in the turret and two Vickers machine-guns mounted in the hull sides. Firepower was in fact partly sacrificed to speed: the Medium Mark II could travel at 15 mph and had a radius of 150 miles; it carried a crew of 5.

Guderian had in the meantime become the leading expert on armour and mechanization in Germany, and by the time that Hitler finally emerged as the German leader after the 1933 putsch, he was in command of a motorized battalion and now in a position to experiment with the theories he had read about and evolved by himself with the help of dummy tanks and guns[1]. There was opposition from within the High Command to these new ideas but it never reached the same proportions as in Britain and France. Hitler attended one of Guderian's demonstrations and was immediately impressed with the potential which the tank offered. The Army was expanded and a significant proportion of the new effort was devoted to creating new armoured, or Panzer, divisions; by 1935 three Panzer divisions were in existence and more were planned.

In the United States the National Defence Act of 1920 eliminated the wartime tank corps and merged tanks with infantry; the budget for tanks that year was 500 dollars. Many good officers and men deserted a lost cause and tank doctrine as such sank into oblivion. Not surprisingly the US Army, now sheltering behind illusions of geography and perpetual peace, was little interested in the work of Walter Christie, an American who designed revolutionary suspensions for tanks. Nevertheless a few experimental vehicles using the new suspension were developed: one of these, the M-1931 (or T-3), was years ahead of its time – but it was the Russians, not the Americans, who saw it.

The Russians purchased two of these tanks and from them developed their BT series and eventually the famous T-34. By the early 1930s the Russians had developed a powerful mechanized army which was masterminded by their leading tank expert, Marshal Tukhachevski. A Military Academy of Mechanization and Motorization was established and although Hitler abandoned the Kazan school the Russians continued to develop new tank designs of their own. By 1935 the Soviet Union possessed the largest mechanized force the world had seen, but the Stalin purges which followed decimated the ranks of 'progressive' officers. The old cavalry diehards now filled the vacuum left by Tukhachevski, the mechanized corps were disbanded and the tank was relegated to the subordinate task of co-operating with the rifle divisions.

[1] Guderian was not a tank theorist of long standing. His ideas on mobility and mechanization first took root when he was a staff officer with the Army Transport Service. Remarkably, he did not see his first tank until 1929, when he visited Sweden.

OPPOSITE *After the Treaty of Versailles many armoured vehicles in Germany were transformed into agricultural machines, here on show at the Berlin Exhibition, 1920.*

THIS PAGE *Germany built up new armour stocks through secret deals with Sweden and the Russians who, in 1930, bought a British Carden Loyd light tank*

(below is a Mark II) and from it developed the Pzkw Mark I; in the picture above a detachment of Mark I Panzers parades before Hitler on his birthday in 1937.

THIS PAGE AND OPPOSITE, TOP While the Americans saw little use for the highly advanced designs of Walter Christie, whose M-1931 tank is shown in the top picture opposite, the Russians were greatly impressed. They bought two of the tanks and from them developed their BT series. In the picture above BT-7-2 tanks are shown parading at the Kiev manoeuvres in 1935. The BT series led, in turn, to the famous T-34 tank (seen below and on pages 78-79).

OPPOSITE, RIGHT In another surge of engineering enterprise the Russians produced their T-26 light tank (top picture in sequence) after studying the Vickers 6-ton type (centre without guns); below is the Russian T-37 amphibious tank.

Meanwhile in both Britain and France the tank was still low on the list of priorities. The French relied for their salvation on the fortification of the Maginot Line and the British were chiefly gripped by an exaggerated faith in the power of the bomber – although they had in principle accepted mechanization as a substitute for horse cavalry. Britain had four major vehicle types: the tankette for machine-gun and mortar, the light tank (Vickers Mark IV) for reconnaissance, the cruiser tank (A–9 and A–10) for cavalry exploitation, and the infantry tank for close infantry co-operation. An armoured division was established in 1937 and was equipped with the cruiser and light tanks. These machines, however, emphasized mobility rather than firepower, which severely restricted their capabilities. Their introduction reflected the current thinking of Elles, then Master-General of Ordnance. He had earlier been convinced that the anti-tank gun was superior to the tank and so had opposed any development of heavier armour along the lines the Germans had taken. But by 1930 he had begun to relent a little and in that year had ordered a new heavy infantry tank from Vickers (the firm which alone had survived the rigours of the inter-war years and now had a monopoly). Working to a strict budget Vickers produced the Infantry Tank Mark I: this had heavy armour protection but in other respects, with only a two-man crew and a machine-gun for the main armament, it was quite inadequate for combat. Nevertheless it went into quantity production and a battalion of the Royal Tank Corps took it to France in 1939. It was closely followed by the Mark II, better known as the Matilda; this was a bigger tank which possessed the same degree of protection and was armed with the excellent 2-pounder (or 40-mm) cannon.

Guderian's Panzers did not make the same mistakes as the British; even so, their main tank, still the Panzer Mark I, was more suited to training than to combat. But new tanks were planned and at least the armoured divisions contained infantry and support formations capable of operating at the speed of the tanks. As early as 1935 Guderian had seen the need for a medium tank armed with a 75-mm gun and shortly afterwards work began on the Mark IV tank, the last German tank to be developed before the war. In the meantime the Mark II, armed with a 20-mm gun, and the Mark III, which had a short-barrelled 50-mm gun, began to appear in the armoured divisions in increasing numbers.

The British, on the other hand, were totally committed to the 2-pounder gun which, though excellent at the time, could not fire high explosive. Later this was to be a major tactical disadvantage against the anti-tank guns of the Afrika Korps, and when the need arose for a bigger gun, the British had to start again from the beginning and redesign their armour. The failure of her tank policy in the late 1930s in fact meant that it was 1944 before Britain was able to deploy a medium tank with a 75-mm gun of indigenous manufacture.

Between 1935 and 1937 a bitter controversy raged in the German High Command over the future role of armour. General Beck, the Chief of Staff, wanted to follow the French precedent of deploying tanks in close support of infantry. But this misguided theory – which was, incidentally, to prove fatal for France in 1940 – was successfully combated by Guderian, who expounded his theories in a book, *Achtung Panzer*, and went on to form the Panzer Corps composed of a Panzer division and a motorized infantry division.

The theories which had developed about armour during the inter-war years had their true baptism in the Spanish Civil War (1936–39). The Russians dispatched more than 700 tanks – mostly of the Christie and Vickers types – to support the Republicans. The Germans, who supported Franco and the Nationalists, equipped the Kondor Legion with the Mark I, while the Italians sent tankettes in the same cause. Neither side used its armour properly, but the Germans for their part learned many valuable lessons in the use of tactical air support.

The Russians, however, learned still more in Manchuria during a series of border clashes with Japan. There, in August 1939, a little-known tank general called Zhukov inflicted a major defeat on the Japanese at Khalkhin Gol in what was to become a blueprint operation for his great victories over the Germans at Stalingrad and Kursk.

OPPOSITE The Spanish Civil War (1935–39) was a major proving ground for Russian and German armour. Here Russian tanks press into Teruel (above) after it had fallen to the Republicans. Below, rebel troops examine a captured Russian tank on the outskirts of Madrid.

RIGHT Still more valuable to the Russians was the experience they gained against the Japanese in Manchuria in mid-1939. A new hero of the armoured divisions then emerged – G. K. Zhukov – seen here when he was commander of the Don Cossack division in 1935.

BELOW Soviet infantrymen in Manchuria advance with tank cover at Khalkhin Gol, scene of Zhukov's first significant victory.

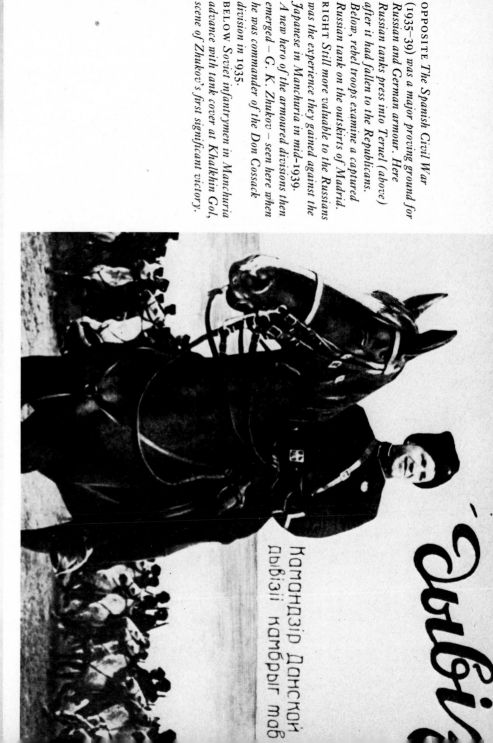

командир Донской дывізіі камбриг таб

On the eve of World War II none of the main protagonists had cause to feel completely satisfied with the quality of its tank formations. The French had belatedly entered the race and had 3,000 modern tanks deployed for war. Their industry, though plagued by Communist agitation, had made notable progress in armour production. The light mechanized divisions were equipped with the fast 20-ton Somua, armed with a 47-mm gun, while the heavy tank formations were equipped with the Char B, a 34-ton monster with a 47-mm cannon in the turret and a 75-mm howitzer in the front of the hull. Although both tanks

suffered tactical limitations because of their one-man turrets it was generally agreed that the Somua was one of the best tanks in any country at the start of the war. In terms of doctrine, however, French ideas were sadly backward: the bulk of the armour was still tied to the apron strings of the infantry while the three light mechanized divisions (each with 220 tanks and a brigade of infantry) inherited the tactics of the old French light cavalry and were deployed as a screen to the main body of the armies as, now on the very brink of hostilities, they advanced into Belgium.

French armour was relatively strong at the outbreak of World War II. France's best tanks were the Somua (opposite, above), a fast 20-ton vehicle armed with a 47-mm gun, and the giant Char B (below) which weighed 34 tons and carried a 47-mm gun in the turret and a 75-mm howitzer in the front of the hull. Another French type was the Renault R-35 (above), a 9.8-ton light tank mounting a 37-mm gun which in some units of the French Army replaced the old FT models of World War I vintage.

Even the Panzers, the élite of the Wehrmacht, were still a long way from Guderian's concept of a balanced armoured force: the infantry and support elements still lacked their armoured half-tracks and the supply units were road-bound. There were six Panzer divisions and four light divisions, making a total of 3,195 tanks, and it was they that spearheaded the advance of 44 divisions into Poland on 1 September 1939. The Luftwaffe easily achieved total air superiority and the ill-equipped Polish Army reeled back before the full onslaught of Blitzkrieg. The Poles had few tanks or anti-tank guns and though their massed brigades of horse cavalry charged the German tanks with suicidal bravery there was little they could do to prevent the invasion and swift overrunning of their country.

On the one side in 1939 stood the brave squadrons of Polish horse cavalry (opposite). On the other were the German dive-bombers which rapidly claimed command of the air and so could give virtually unrestricted support to their Panzer divisions on the ground.

The Tanks at War 1939–1945

A Chronology

THE SYMBOL ☐ DENOTES ACTIVITY OVER A PERIOD OF TIME

1939

SEPTEMBER
1   Germany invades Poland in first Blitzkrieg campaign.
3   Britain and France declare war on Germany.
17   Soviet invasion of Poland.
28   Surrender of Warsaw. Russo-German treaty partitions Poland.

OCTOBER
10   First attempt by German submarines to implement wolf-pack tactics in Atlantic.
12   First divisions of British Expeditionary Force join Allied line at Lille.

NOVEMBER
4   Repeal of US Neutrality Law; materials of war sold to Britain on cash-and-carry basis.
30   Soviet invasion of Finland; capitulates on 12 March.

1940

APRIL
9   Germany occupies Denmark; landings at six cities in Norway.
10   First Battle of Narvik; Second Battle on 13th.

MAY
10   Germany invades France and Low Countries in second major Blitzkrieg operation.
15   Panzer breakthrough on Meuse front.
26   Start of Dunkirk evacuation (Operation Dynamo); completed on 4 June.
☐   Germans begin up-gunning of Marks III and IV tanks to 50-mm and 75-mm high velocity guns respectively.

JUNE
4   Start of Allied evacuation of Norway; completed on 10th.
10   Italy joins war on Germany's side.
14   Germans enter Paris; armistice signed on 22nd.

JULY
10   Battle of Britain begins.
16   Hitler issues directive for plan to invade Britain (Operation Sea Lion).

SEPTEMBER
17   Operation Sea Lion indefinitely postponed after failure of Luftwaffe to defeat RAF.
27   Axis pact signed in Berlin by Germany, Italy and Japan.

OCTOBER
28   Italians invade Greece.

DECEMBER
9   General O'Connor leads Western Desert Force with 275 tanks against Italians at Sidi Barrani.

1941

FEBRUARY
6–7   Fall of Benghazi, 20,000 Italians surrender.
12   General Rommel arrives in Tripoli.

MARCH
11   Passing of Lend Lease Act by USA.
24   Rommel begins first offensive at El Agheila; encircles Tobruk on 13 April.

APRIL
6   German invasion of Yugoslavia and Greece; Allies begin evacuation of Greece on 22nd.

JUNE
22   Germany invades USSR (Operation Barbarossa).

JULY
9   Minsk falls to German armoured pincer; Smolensk taken on 15th.
24   Japan secures 'protection rights' from France over Indo-China.
☐   Lee-Grant M-3 tanks put into quantity production to give Allies a tank with a 75-mm gun.

JULY–AUGUST
   Hitler switches main offensive away from Moscow to Ukraine.

SEPTEMBER
8   Leningrad cut off by German tanks.
19   Fall of Kiev.
26   Moscow offensive resumed; progress slowed by onset of winter.

OCTOBER
21   General Zhukov takes command of Moscow's outer defences.

NOVEMBER–DECEMBER
8   Defence of Moscow and beginning of Russian counter-offensive.
☐   General Auchinleck's desert offensive pushes Rommel back to El Agheila (ends 31 December).

DECEMBER
7   Japanese attack Pearl Harbour, Malaya and Siam (Thailand).
8   USA declares war.
10   Japanese invade Philippines.
11   Germany and Italy declare war on USA.

1942

JANUARY
9   Russian counter-blows reach Smolensk province.

JANUARY–JULY
☐   Rommel's second desert offensive drives Eighth Army back to El Alamein line (7 July).

FEBRUARY
15   Fall of Singapore to Japanese forces.
☐   Germans stabilize their front in Russia.

APRIL
8   Capitulation of Philippines (except Corregidor, 6 May).

MAY
8   Germans launch spring offensive on Eastern Front.

JUNE
4–6   Battle of Midway.

JULY
6   Germans take Voronezh; Hitler orders drive on Stalingrad and Caucasus.

AUGUST
7   US landings on Guadalcanal; island cleared in February 1943.
13   General Montgomery takes over command of Eighth Army.
24   Battle of Stalingrad begins.
31   Battle of Alam Halfa begins. Montgomery deploys tanks in hull-down positions and fends off Rommel (withdraws 7 September).

SEPTEMBER
☐   German Tiger tanks receive premature baptism on Leningrad front.
☐   Japanese offensive in New Guinea halted by Australians.

OCTOBER
23   Battle of El Alamein begins. Sherman M-4 tanks supplied for first time to British crews. Axis front crumbles on 4 November.

NOVEMBER
8   Anglo-American landings in North Africa (Operation Torch). US forces equipped with bazookas.
19–23   Soviet counter-attack at Stalingrad; German Sixth Army cut off.
20   Siege of Malta lifted.

1943

FEBRUARY
2   German Sixth Army surrenders in Stalingrad.

FEBRUARY–MARCH
□ General von Manstein organizes German counter-offensive, recaptures Kharkov on 14 March.

MAY
3–13 Battle of Tunisia ends Axis presence in North Africa.

JUNE
□ US and British begin combined bomber offensive against Germany.

JULY
4–16 Kursk – biggest ever tank battle. German 'Elefant' SP gun makes disastrous début; Panthers also appear for first time.

10 Allied landings in Sicily.

JULY–NOVEMBER
□ Russian armour drives Germans beyond Smolensk (25 September) and Kiev (6 November); Seventeenth Army cut off in Crimea.

SEPTEMBER
3 Allied landings in mainland Italy.

NOVEMBER
1 US landings on Bougainville; Tarawa invaded on 20th using specialized armoured assault vehicles (LVTs).

DECEMBER
□ First batch of new Russian T-34 tanks, strengthened and up-gunned to 85 mm, come off production line.

1944

JANUARY
20 Allied landings at Anzio, Italy.

JUNE
6 Allied invasion of Normandy (Operation Overlord) using specialized amphibious and assault armour (the 'Funnies').

JULY
21 US landings on Guam.

AUGUST
1 General Patton's Third Army breaks out of Cherbourg peninsula.
15 Allied landings in south of France.
25 Liberation of Paris.

DECEMBER
8 Start of US pre-invasion bombardment of Iwo Jima.
16 Hitler launches Ardennes counter-offensive, delaying Allied advance for six weeks.

1945

FEBRUARY
13–14 Bombing of Dresden.
16 First US carrier raids on Japan.

MARCH
7 US 9th Armoured Division seizes Remagen Bridge and makes first Allied crossing of Rhine.

APRIL
1 US landings on Okinawa; cleared 21 June.
16 Russian guns fire on Berlin.
□ Allied Pershing and Comet tanks arrive to join pursuit across Germany.

MAY
8 Unconditional German surrender.

AUGUST
6/9 Atomic bombing of Japan.
8 USSR declares war on Japan.

SEPTEMBER
2 Japanese instrument of surrender signed aboard US battleship *Missouri* in Tokyo Bay.

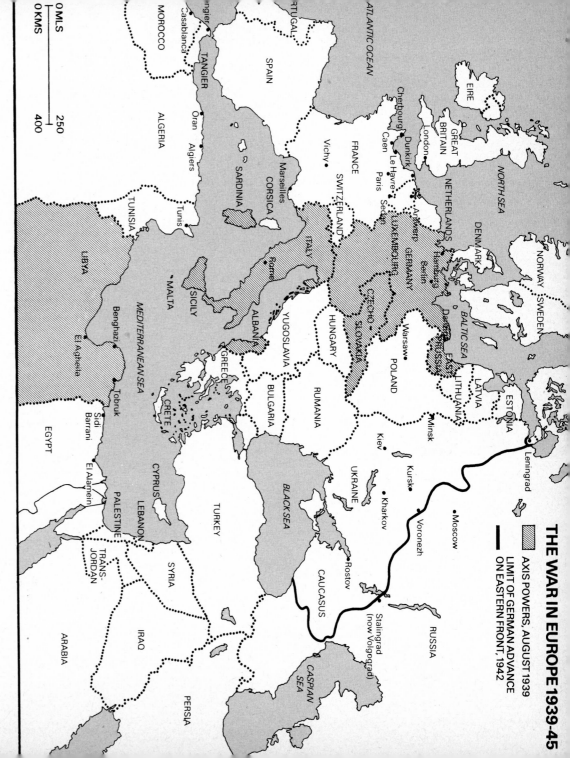

THE WAR IN EUROPE 1939-45

▨ AXIS POWERS, AUGUST 1939
▬ LIMIT OF GERMAN ADVANCE ON EASTERN FRONT, 1942

0 MLS 250
0 KMS 400

Chapter Four

Blitzkrieg in the West

indifferently armed and tactically out of date, and its morale, which had never really recovered from the shock of the Great War, had since been undermined by political intrigue. In the face of a bold adversary, equipped with novel tactics, willing to take all risks and convinced of its superiority, the French Army was tailormade for disaster.

The whole Blitzkrieg campaign hinged on the employment of armour and was essentially a clash of principles between two rival schools. The Allies outnumbered the Germans in armour but believed in distributing their tanks in fairly even proportions along the entire front; the Panzers, massed in corps formations, were therefore assured of local superiority at the point of impact. The Allies, furthermore, were convinced that the tank could not defeat the anti-tank gun: this, they thought, could only be achieved by the infantry and artillery. But the point was missed that infantry and artillery should be made more mobile. The British Expeditionary Force was the most mobile in Europe but it had only 229 tanks of which 171 were useless light tanks. Neither the British nor the French were capable of deploying adequate air cover for their ground forces and this failure left their armies horribly exposed to the Luftwaffe.

The Allied plan of operations (Plan D), designed to counter a German invasion of France and the Low Countries, gave itself away. It was impossible to launch four Allied armies into Belgium at a moment's notice without providing the German High Command with food for thought. The Germans deduced the likely Allied moves and made their own plans accordingly. After a series of false alarms, when planned offensives were postponed because of bad weather, the Germans drew up their final plan[1] secure in their knowledge of the enemy's; thus the battle of wits was already half won. To achieve the necessary surprise, the Germans simply struck the Allied lines where they were least expected. The French deployed to meet what they thought would be the main blow north of Namur through the Gembloux Gap; the Germans struck south of Namur and advanced on the Ardennes Forest, which the French considered impenetrable by armour.

General Heinz Guderian, a master of tank strategy, who led the Panzer breakthrough at Sedan.

In May 1940 the British and French armies were as ill-prepared for the German Blitzkrieg as their erstwhile Polish allies had been the previous summer. However, to foreigners in general, and to Englishmen in particular, the French Army was accepted as the most formidable in Europe – even though in reality it was nothing of the kind. It was

The Germans proved that it could be penetrated in force and at speed. The Ardennes was undoubtedly a formidable obstacle but like any natural barrier it could be conquered if preparations were sufficiently thorough.

General Gamelin and the French High Command similarly felt that the River Meuse could not be crossed without a lengthy build-up of weapons, supplies and man-power. But the Germans planned this phase of the operation

with the same infinite care as they took over the Ardennes. They chose to make their greatest effort on a 50-mile front between Houx-Dinant and Sedan against the weak Series B divisions of the French Ninth and Second Armies; composed almost entirely of reservists and men over 40 years of age, these were poorly equipped, had little motor transport and were almost defenceless against either air or

power. And at speed. The Ardennes was undoubtedly a formidable obstacle but like any natural barrier it could be conquered if preparations were sufficiently thorough.

tank assaults.

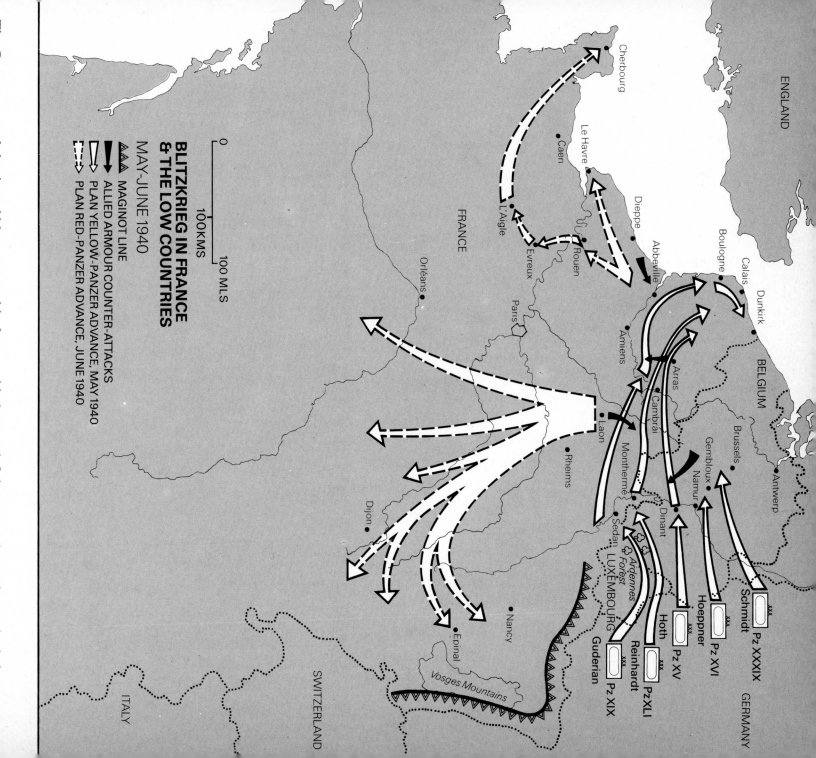

BLITZKRIEG IN FRANCE & THE LOW COUNTRIES

MAY–JUNE 1940

△△△ MAGINOT LINE
⟱ ALLIED ARMOUR COUNTER-ATTACKS
⟱ PLAN YELLOW-PANZER ADVANCE, MAY 1940
⬇ PLAN RED-PANZER ADVANCE, JUNE 1940

0   100KMS

100 MLS

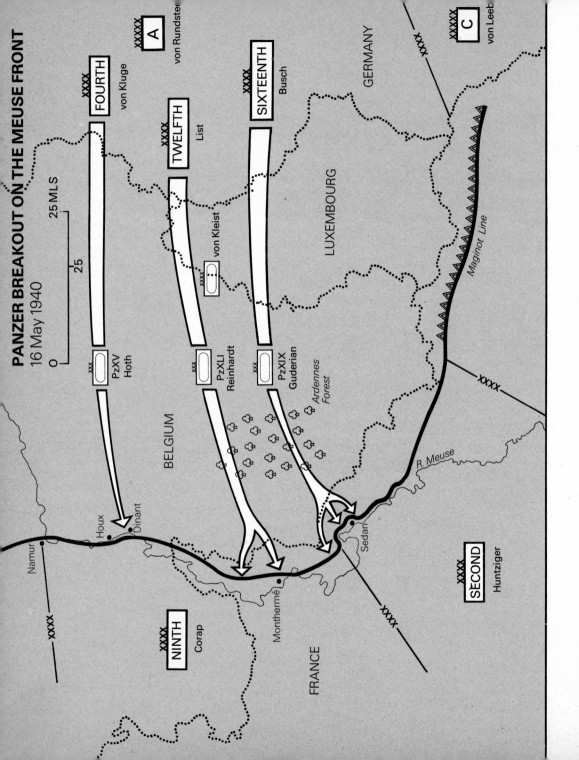

PANZER BREAKOUT ON THE MEUSE FRONT
16 May 1940

0   25   25 MLS

FOURTH
von Kluge
xxxx
A
von Rundste

xxx
PzXV
Hoth

TWELFTH
List
xxxx

xxx
PzXLI
Reinhardt

von Kleist
xxxx

SIXTEENTH
Busch
xxxx

xxx
PzXIX
Guderian

BELGIUM

Namur

Houx
Dinant

Monthermé

Ardennes Forest

LUXEMBOURG

GERMANY

Maginot Line

R. Meuse

Sedan

NINTH
Corap
xxxx

FRANCE

SECOND
Huntziger
xxxx

C
von Leeb
xxxxx

Within this front the blows fell at Sedan, Monthermé and Houx, but of these Sedan was the most vital. The city was pivot to a road and rail network that radiated out to the coast, towards Paris, and south behind the Maginot Line; once taken, the opportunities it offered for exploitation were boundless.

The German advance began on 10 May 1940. While the Allied armies hurried north-east to cover Brussels and what they believed to be the main threat, the German Panzers broke through the thin crust of light mechanized units in the Ardennes and on 12 May emerged on the east bank of the Meuse. The decisive part of this operation was entrusted to von Kleist's Group, comprising five Panzer and three motorized divisions further subdivided into two Panzer corps commanded by Reinhardt at Monthermé and Guderian at Sedan. On the morning of 13 May the French infantry was subjected to an air blitz of terrifying proportions while the Panzers deployed off the line of march for the river crossing. At first the French infantry put up a stubborn resistance and three out of the seven crossings attempted by the Germans failed completely; but the other

62

four eventually succeeded after rather shaky starts. Two French armoured divisions were in a position to intervene at that point but there was a terrible muddle in their movement orders with the result that they were never committed to the battle properly and became engulfed in the general chaos and confusion as the front collapsed. (There is, furthermore, no evidence of French GHQ being informed of the nature of the German offensive on the Meuse Front until 16 May.)

After an initial and quite unnecessary halt while the German High Command drew breath, the Panzers fanned out and drove hard for the coast. Their tactics were not new: the Panzers emphasized speed and mobility and simply outflanked or bypassed isolated pockets of resistance in their dash westwards. The French for their part had no general strategic reserve which could deploy against the breakthrough, most of their reserve formations being concentrated behind the Maginot Line.

OPPOSITE Successor to the German Marks I and II was the more powerful Mark III mounting the short 50-mm gun. RIGHT Tank production line at Krupp's.

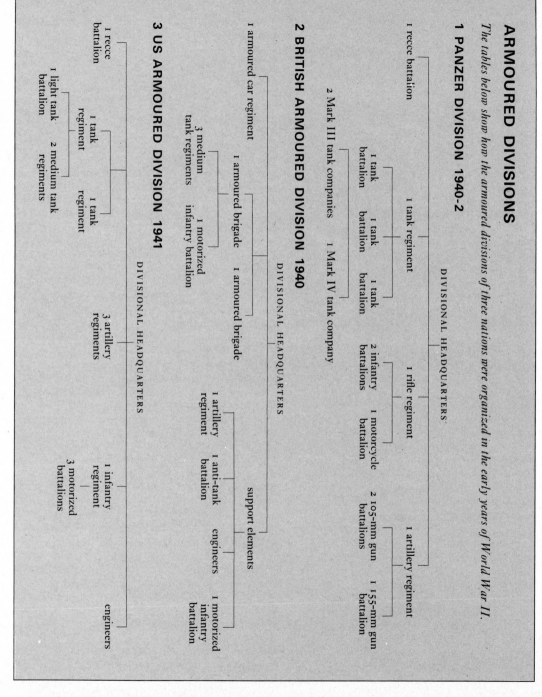

ARMOURED DIVISIONS

The tables below show how the armoured divisions of three nations were organized in the early years of World War II.

1 PANZER DIVISION 1940-2

DIVISIONAL HEADQUARTERS

- 1 recce battalion
- 1 tank regiment
  - 1 tank battalion
  - 1 tank battalion
- 1 rifle regiment
  - 2 infantry battalions
  - 1 motorcycle battalion
- 1 artillery regiment
  - 2 105-mm gun battalions
  - 1 155-mm gun battalion

2 BRITISH ARMOURED DIVISION 1940

DIVISIONAL HEADQUARTERS

- 1 armoured car regiment
- 1 armoured brigade
  - 3 medium tank regiments
  - 1 motorized infantry battalion
- 1 armoured brigade
  - 2 Mark III tank companies
  - 1 Mark IV tank company
- 1 artillery regiment
  - 1 anti-tank battalion
- support elements
  - engineers

3 US ARMOURED DIVISION 1941

DIVISIONAL HEADQUARTERS

- 1 recce battalion
- 1 tank regiment
  - 1 light tank battalion
  - 2 medium tank regiments
- 1 tank regiment
  - 3 medium tank regiments
- 3 artillery regiments
- 1 infantry regiment
  - 3 motorized battalions
- 1 motorized infantry battalion
- engineers

63

was that the German overreacted to the British counter-attack, ordered the Panzers to halt at Arras and in their present positions on the coast, and forbade any move north-eastwards to Dunkirk. This gave Gort just enough time to garrison the perimeter and thus safeguard his rear areas. Behind this secure defence he was able to organize an orderly evacuation of his beleaguered forces (Operation Dynamo), which took place between 26 May and 4 June.

Much has been written about the failure of the Panzers to complete what many have since regarded as the objective of the operation, the complete destruction of the Allied armies. General Halder, the German Chief of Staff, claimed that it was Hitler who 'prevented the complete destruction of the British Army by withdrawing the German tanks which were already to their rear'. Von Rundstedt, then Colonel-General commanding Army Group A, said after the war that he had wanted three Panzer divisions to complete the operation but this was forbidden by Hitler, an act which he described as an 'incredible blunder'. But the conquest of France was not yet complete and the tanks needed time to refit before they could be ready for their part in Plan Red and the advance southwards across the Somme to Paris and the Mediter-ranean. Moreover Marshal Goering and the Luftwaffe convinced Hitler that they could bombard the Allies into capitulation, while it was Guderian himself who on 28 May made a personal report to Hitler that the terrain around Dunkirk was totally unsuited to tanks. More fundamentally, it is also as well to remember that the German commanders had been weaned on von Clausewitz and the principles of a 'Continental' strategy, and in consequence had failed to anticipate an evacuation by sea.

It was, therefore, German indecision, coupled with the sterling qualities of the British fighting soldier and the magnificent co-operation of the Royal Navy and Air Force, which resulted in more than a third of a million Allied soldiers being evacuated from the beaches and port of Dunkirk. Although the Panzers failed in the last analysis to achieve a decisive victory they had nevertheless demon-strated to the world the true potential of Blitzkrieg when the defence allowed it freedom to operate. Lord Gort in his despatches said:

The speed with which the enemy exploited his penetration of the French Front, his willingness to accept risks to further his aim, and his exploitation of every success to the uttermost limits emphasized even more fully than in the campaigns of the past the advantage which accrues to the commander who knows how best to use time and make time his servant and not his master.

After Dunkirk there were fewer than 200 battleworthy tanks available for the defence of Britain. Factories were still a long way short of full production and so the old and medium tanks had to be brought out of retirement and deployed alongside the A-10 cruisers and the infantry

The bulk of the Panzer divisions was still made up of Mark I and Mark II tanks, and by the time the forward elements gazed out over the English Channel at Abbeville on 20 May many vehicles had become casualties through mechanical failure. Altogether at this stage the Panzers had lost about 40% of their strength; nevertheless they had executed the greatest of all flanking movements – the encirclement of the Allied armies in Belgium. The French Premier, Paul Reynaud, sacked Gamelin and recalled Weygand from Syria to try and retrieve what was in fact a hopeless situation. Lord Gort, in command of the British Expeditionary Force, now found his line of communica-tions to the base ports of Cherbourg and Le Havre cut and his rear threatened, and ordered a move back to the Channel port of Dunkirk. This began on 19 May when he sent his chief of staff, General Pownall, back to London to begin preparations for an evacuation.

Weygand had no strategic reserve to block the German penetration and so vainly sought to link up with the northern armies, but events had overtaken and paralysed the High Command. De Gaulle and the newly-created 4th Armoured Division counter-attacked at Laon but this was nothing more than a gesture and did little to alter the course of events. The British created two mixed infantry and armoured units and made a determined attempt to relieve the pressure around their main base at Arras on 21 May. At first the lumbering Matildas caused havoc as they caught Rommel's Panzers in the flank but the Germans quickly retrieved their situation and, from a tactical point of view, the operation failed. On a strategic level, however, its significance was more profound, for the audacity of the German Panzers had to a certain extent unnerved the German High Command, which became increasingly concerned with the vulnerability of its over-extended forces and feared a repetition of the Marne reversal of 1914. The result

Matildas. New tanks under production compared favourably with the Panzers for speed and armour but were already lagging behind in the vital aspect of gunpower. Rough treatment at the hands of the Matilda and Char B had hastened the German conversion to tanks with 50-mm and 75-mm high-velocity guns, while the British had only the now obsolescent 2-pounder (or 40-mm). There was a new British tank gun, the 6-pounder (57-mm), but to have put this into production would have resulted in delays at a time when any gun was better than no gun at all. The necessary programmes in research and development were curtailed and untried tanks were rushed into quantity production. In real terms this meant producing obsolete equipment while cutting back on the development of the next generation; thus by sacrificing quality Britain surrendered her parity and the chance of ever recovering the lead over the Germans in tank design and construction.

A neutral United States had watched with alarm as events unfurled in Europe and an immediate expansion was ordered in her armed forces. However, in terms of the tank the locust years of the inter-war period had left an indelible mark and the United States was forced merely to emulate others. The new armoured formations were centred on Fort Knox, where the 7th Cavalry formed the nucleus of the 1st Armoured Division, an exact replica of the Panzers in its complement of tanks and infantry. But the only tank in production was the cruiser M-2 A-1, armed with a 37-mm gun; to meet the immediate need for a battle tank the Americans were therefore forced to adapt the experimental T-5 E-2, mounting a 75-mm gun in a side sponson.

USA W-30444

The Desert War

While the USA watched from the sidelines, the Western Desert of North Africa was already providing the next arena for the clash of armour. The Western Desert region is really one of limestone, with little real desert, and stretches for 1,400 miles between the terminal ports of Tripoli to the west and Alexandria to the east. A German general, von Ravenstein, described it as 'a tactician's paradise and a quartermaster's hell', for there was only one natural defence line between El Agheila and El Alamein and except for the coast road the entire zone was devoid of communications. Thus the farther a force advanced, the more its supply lines were extended and the weaker it became, as well as increasingly vulnerable to counter blows from the opposing side.

The first Western Desert campaign lasted from the autumn of 1940 to February 1941. During this period the Allied Western Desert Force under General O'Connor at first countered a tepid invasion by Marshal Graziani and the Italians and then swung into a brilliantly co-ordinated offensive which carried the British beyond Benghazi. The Italians could find no answer to O'Connor's bold use of tanks as Tobruk and Derna fell and a vast booty was left behind the retreating Italians. The three principal tanks which featured in these early months were the British Crusader, the American Stuart (or 'Honey', as it was called

by its British crews) and the Italian M-13/40. Each represented entirely different design concepts, but superficially there was little to choose between them, except that the Italian tank was slower than the other two. The Crusader was desperately weak mechanically, however, and its tendency to break down under combat conditions inspired little confidence in it. In contrast the Stuart and the M-13/40 were seeing action after a long period of peacetime development, and although they were adequate at first they too were to fail against the greater protection and hitting power of their later opponents. The high speed and elusive characteristics of the Stuart were no substitute for thicker armour and a bigger gun when action had to be pressed.

For a short while the Matilda infantry tank enjoyed a reputation as a queen of the desert – until it was humbled by the anti-tank guns of the Afrika Korps in the Halfaya Pass. Another British tank was the Valentine: designed by Vickers on St Valentine's Day, 1938, it was a robust tank intended for infantry support but was almost invariably used in the Western Desert in a cruiser role. It was originally armed with the 40-mm gun and was then successfully up-gunned to 57-mm; but by 1943 the Valentine was obsolescent and the chassis were converted for specialized roles and to make self-propelled guns.

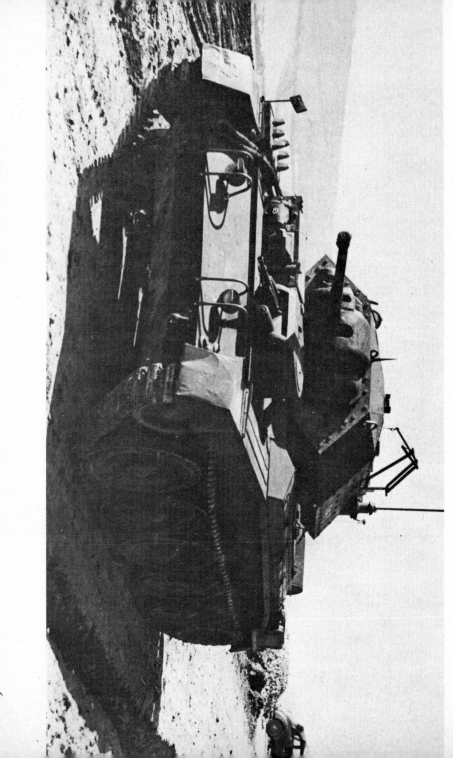

OPPOSITE British tanks stand on an Egyptian quayside in October 1940 in readiness for the desert campaign. In the background is the cruiser HMS York.

ABOVE Italian tank crews stand easy in front of a group of M-13/40 tanks. The latter was one of the principal types used in North Africa.

BELOW A British Crusader tank, mechanically unreliable but a type that saw considerable service in the early stages of the desert fighting.

Panzers of the Afrika Korps swirl in a haze of dust past a captured British bren-gun carrier. Rommel's superior tactics, using his armour in concentrated forces to destroy the British piecemeal, brought him a series of notable victories in the spring of 1941 and later in the first half of 1942.

After the headlong advance described above and the defeat of large elements of the Italian Army at Beda Fomm, O'Connor was poised ready to strike further west and capture the last enemy strongholds before Tripoli. However, his commander-in-chief, General Wavell, was ordered by London to send substantial reinforcements to the Balkans, and O'Connor was left holding Cyrenaica with just one infantry division and a raw armoured brigade for support. In the circumstances this force seemed capable of containing any Italian initiative, but unbeknown to the British Rommel and the advance elements of his Afrika Korps began to disembark at Tripoli in February 1941. Within a few short weeks the Germans completed their preparations and launched a major offensive against the unsuspecting British. The British 2nd Armoured Brigade was caught off balance, outmanoeuvred and destroyed; the infantry fell back in disarray beyond Benghazi, Tobruk was invested and O'Connor captured.

The Afrika Korps then secured a series of brilliant tactical victories over the British, not through over-whelming strength of superior equipment but because it was a few vital degrees more advanced in its tactics and leadership. In the German view everything centred around the mobility and co-ordination of tanks and artillery. In the open desert unmotorized infantry was powerless unless it was protected by tanks, while even mechanized infantry was obliged to scurry from one area of tank-cleared country to the next.

This type of mobile warfare was never really understood by the succession of infantry-orientated British Army generals who held command in the Western Desert. Such generals had been educated in the halcyon days of the late 1930s, when the Staff Colleges emphasized the necessity of destroying the enemy's main forces as the prime objective on the battlefield. In the Western Desert this was interpreted to mean the destruction of enemy armour first – as a preliminary to the main battle. As a result numerically superior forces of British tanks scoured the desert in widely scattered groups while Rommel concentrated his Panzers and destroyed the British in batches. On those occasions when the Panzers were outnumbered they would retire behind a screen of cunningly concealed anti-tank

guns which in turn would take a heavy toll of the British tanks as they charged headlong into the trap. The British commanders never seemed to learn that an enemy tank force does not present itself as a simple objective in battle; because of its mobility its position is not static like that of infantry, and therefore the only real opportunity to destroy it is indirectly, by drawing it out of cover to retrieve a threatened key point. In conversation with a captured British general, Rommel was recorded as saying: 'What difference does it make if you have two tanks to my one when you spread them out and let me smash them in detail?' He subsequently admitted that it was the British artillery which caused him the most trouble – on the odd occasions when it could deploy in support of armour.

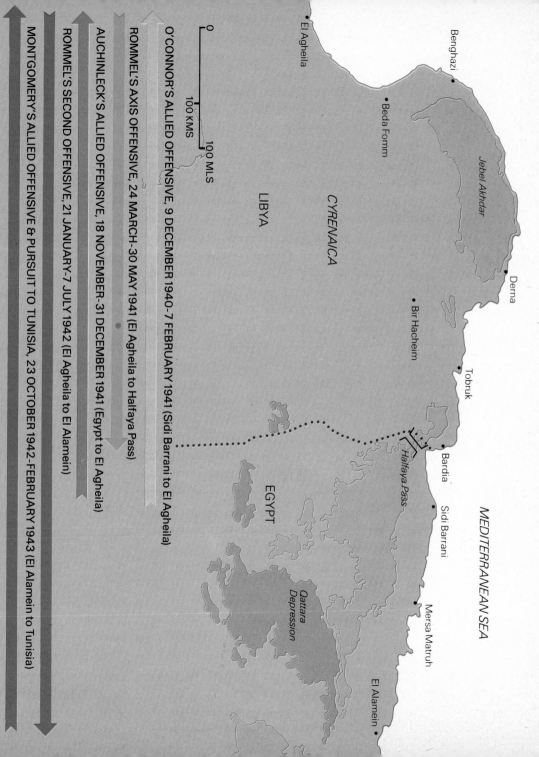

0
100 KMS

0
100 MLS

MEDITERRANEAN SEA

Benghazi

El Agheila

Beda Fomm

Jebel Akhdar

Derna

CYRENAICA

LIBYA

Bir Hacheim

Tobruk

Halfaya Pass

Bardia

Sidi Barrani

Mersa Matruh

EGYPT

Qattara Depression

El Alamein

O'CONNOR'S ALLIED OFFENSIVE, 9 DECEMBER 1940-7 FEBRUARY 1941 (Sidi Barrani to El Agheila)

ROMMEL'S AXIS OFFENSIVE, 24 MARCH-30 MAY 1941 (El Agheila to Halfaya Pass)

AUCHINLECK'S ALLIED OFFENSIVE, 18 NOVEMBER-31 DECEMBER 1941 (Egypt to El Agheila)

ROMMEL'S SECOND OFFENSIVE, 21 JANUARY-7 JULY 1942 (El Agheila to El Alamein)

MONTGOMERY'S ALLIED OFFENSIVE & PURSUIT TO TUNISIA, 23 OCTOBER 1942-FEBRUARY 1943 (El Alamein to Tunisia)

All the British tanks – Valentines, Matildas, Crusaders and Stuarts – were indifferently armed, while in terms of manpower the Italian and German tank crews were on a par with the British veterans and superior to their new formations. The British anti-tank gun was only a 2-pounder and could do little to support its armour or protect its infantry – in contrast to the excellent German 50-mm Pak (Panzerabwehrkanone) anti-tank gun and the 88-mm artillery (though the latter was not as effective in the Western Desert as legend would have us believe).

By the end of 1941 there was a general feeling of inadequacy and disquiet among British tank crews as they bowed before the technical superiority of the Afrika Korps and the mystique which they accorded to Rommel's creative tactical ability. Yet the fundamental feature of such inferiority was the awful inadequacy of British gunpower: the German tanks could kill at 1,000 yards but the British

tanks had to close to 800 yards before they could be sure of getting a decisive hit. Against the German anti-tank guns the British tanks had no high explosive, and their position when there was no artillery or mortar support forthcoming from their infantry was little short of hopeless.

Neither side was ever in a position to inflict a major strategic defeat on the other in the Western Desert throughout most of this period. Britain's dependence for supplies on the long and vulnerable Cape Route, coupled with her bankrupt tactical doctrine, meant that she could never hope to achieve a position of superiority over Rommel. On the German side there were fewer problems of supply but the British still barred the narrow Mediterranean sea routes, while Rommel in any case could never be given sufficient forces to defeat the Eighth Army for as long as Hitler concentrated the main German effort on the Eastern Front, against Russia.

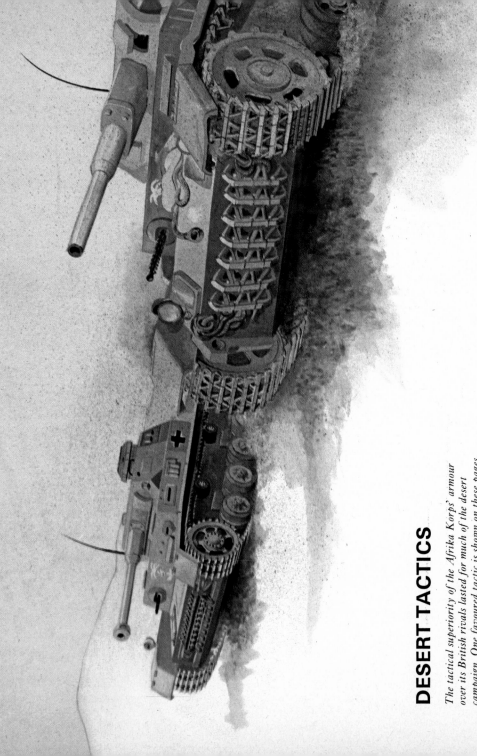

DESERT TACTICS

The tactical superiority of the Afrika Korps' armour over its British rivals lasted for much of the desert campaign. One favoured tactic is shown on these pages. It was used when a German patrol, on making contact with British tanks, found itself outnumbered. It would turn and retire, expecting the British to give chase – which they almost invariably did. The retreating Panzers then drew their enemy across the desert and onto the guns of a concealed and conveniently sited anti-tank screen, where the 50-mm Pak 38s extracted their toll from virtually point-blank range.

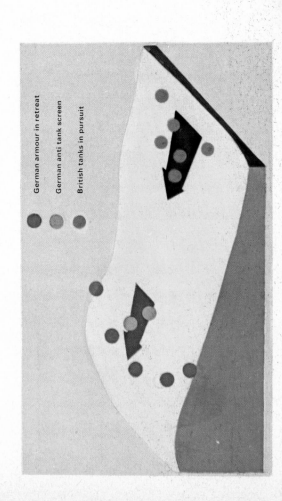

German armour in retreat

German anti tank screen

British tanks in pursuit

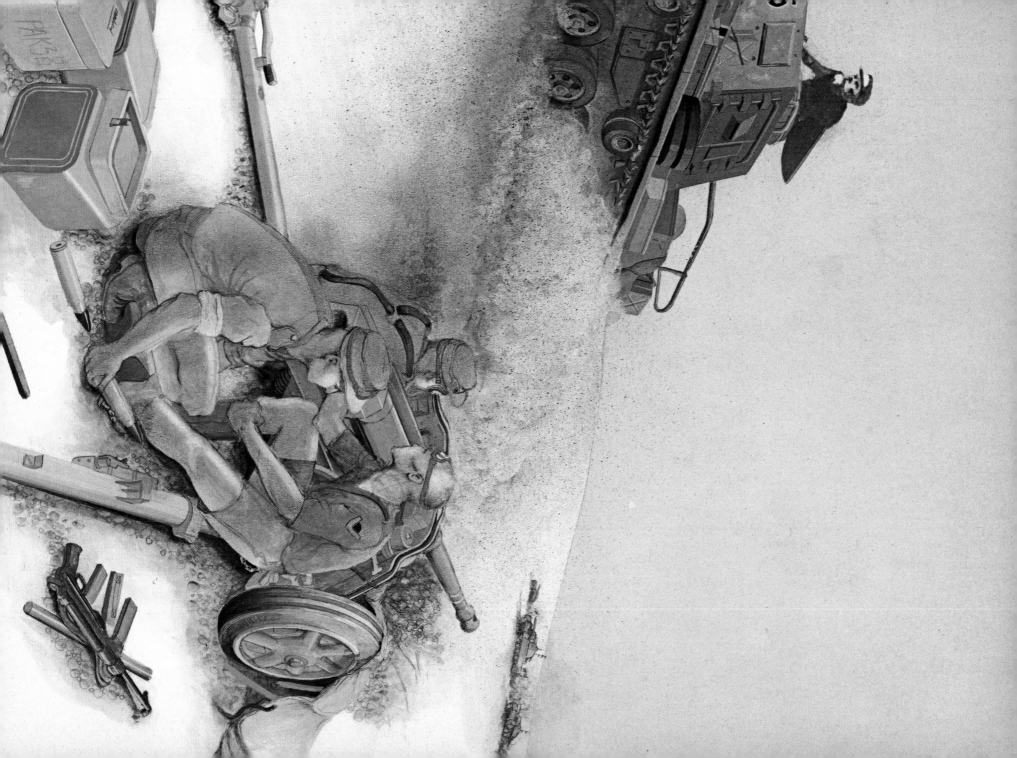

Operation Barbarossa

Directive No. 21, which laid down the guidelines for Operation Barbarossa and the invasion of Russia in June 1941, laid great emphasis on the tank:

The bulk of the Russian Army stationed in 'Western Russia will be destroyed by daring operations led by deeply penetrating armoured spearheads.

Despite the possibly tempting vastness of Russian space, this new German operation in fact had built-in risks which dwarfed the problems earlier confronting the Panzers in France. The main factor in the Panzers' favour was the professionalism and technical excellence of their formations, but their tanks were for the most part the obsolescent Mark III with the short-barrelled 50-mm gun. In relation to the geography of Western Russia the number of Panzers was, moreover, absurdly small (see panel), while their supply formations were to be fatally compromised by the primitive road system. Time, too, was of the very essence since the Panzers, in common with the Wehrmacht in general, were not equipped for winter warfare and in such circumstances the great size of the territory could – and did – tell against them.

The Russians also held a significant advantage that had little to do with geography. This was in the quality of their armour, which produced one of the most startling revelations of the war. The T-34, in particular, rendered obsolete at one stroke all German tank development to date. It was a tank which combined a near-perfect balance between hitting power and self-protection, between long-range mobility and reliability. The broad tracks and low ground-bearing pressure of only 10 pounds per square inch allowed the tank to move across terrain and in weather which immobilized the Panzers. The T-34 was first built in 1939 and was the creation not of any inspirational genius but of the robust common sense of its designer, Mikhail Koshkin, who could envisage the needs of the battlefield with greater clarity than his contemporaries in other countries. In June 1941, as Operation Barbarossa began, there were approximately 1,000 of these tanks available – though initially their value was undermined by the manner in which they were deployed and by the tactical ineptitude of their crews. (In all some 2,400 vehicles occupied the Russian tank parks on the eve of Barbarossa; many of these were, however, obsolete or in a state of disrepair.)

September 1941: three months after the first German hammer-blows, Russian T-40 reconnaissance tanks are loaded for delivery to the front line. The next two months were to be critical for both sides as the fighting neared Moscow.

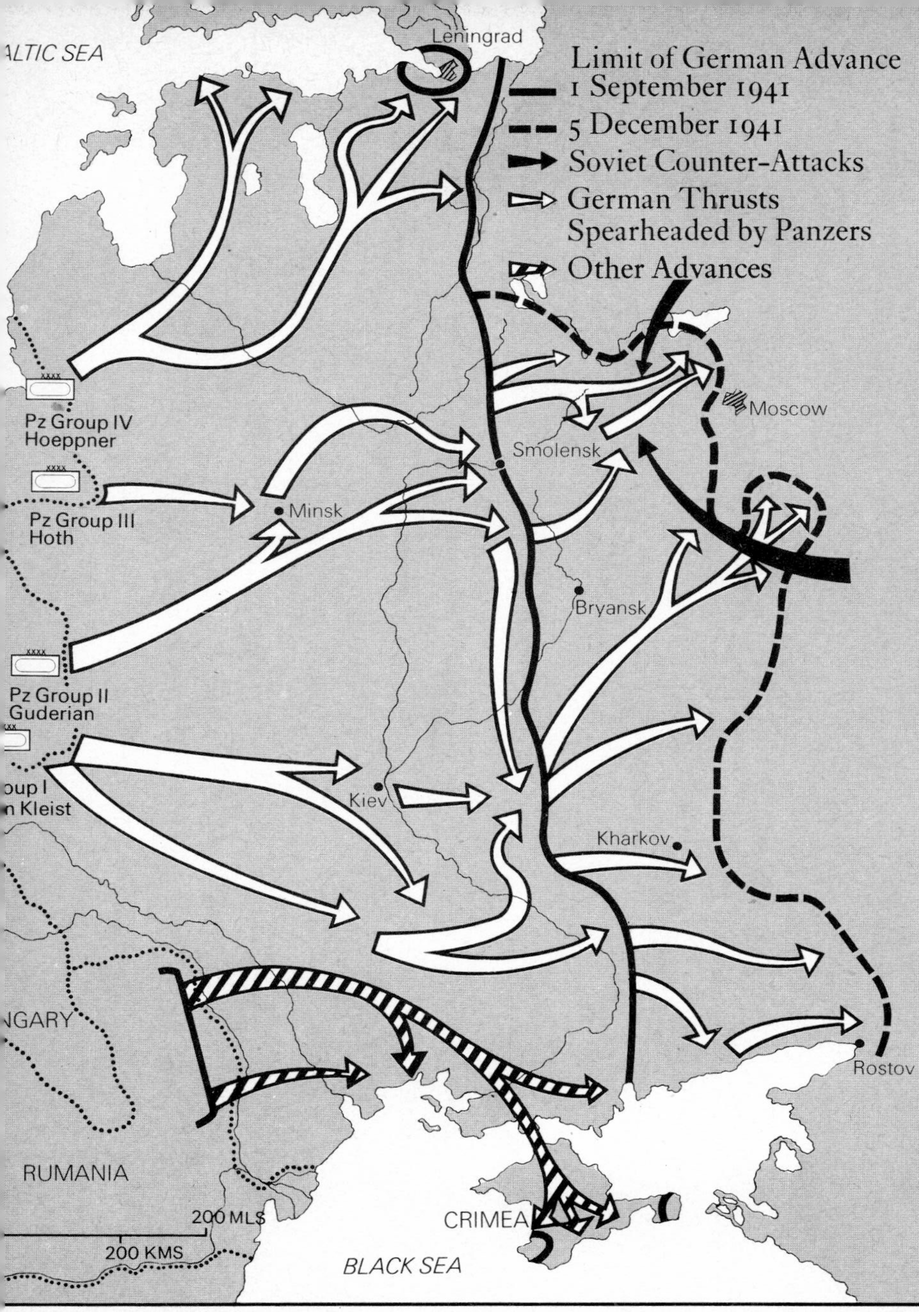
ALTIC SEA
Leningrad
Limit of German Advance
1 September 1941
5 December 1941
Soviet Counter-Attacks
German Thrusts
Spearheaded by Panzers
Other Advances
Pz Group IV
Hoeppner
Pz Group III
Hoth
Pz Group II
Guderian
Moscow
Smolensk
Minsk
Bryansk
Kiev
Kharkov
Rostov
RUMANIA
CRIMEA
BLACK SEA
200 MLS
200 KMS

OPERATION BARBAROSSA
June 1941

GERMAN ORDER OF BATTLE

ARMIES	PANZER DIVISIONS	INFANTRY & OTHER
Army Group North (von Leeb)		
Eighteenth Army (von Kuchler)		8
Fourth Panzer Group (Hoeppner)	3	6
Sixteenth Army (Busch)		12
Reserve		1
Army Group Centre (von Bock)		
Ninth Army (Strauss)		9
Third Panzer Group (Hoth)	4	7
Fourth Army (von Kluge)		16
Second Panzer Group (Guderian)	5	9
Reserve		1
Army Group South (von Rundstedt)		
Sixth Army (von Reichenau)		6
First Panzer Group (von Kleist)	5	9
Seventeenth Army (Stülpnagel)		13
Eleventh Army (Schobert)		7
Rumanian Army (Antonesch)		14
Reserve		3
OKH (Army High Command) Reserve (Brauchitsch)	2	22

German Armoured Strength
OPERATION BARBAROSSA

The meagre German total of 3,196 tanks ready at the beginning of the Operation was made up as follows:

NUMBER OF TANKS	TYPE OF TANK	TYPE OF GUN
1,893	Mark III	Short-barrelled L-42 50-mm
1,132	Mark IV	High-velocity L-43 75-mm
131	Mark II	37-mm
40	Mark III	Long-barrelled L-60 50-mm

RUSSIAN T-34/76

The T-34 earned its reputation as the greatest tank produced in World War II because it outgunned and outmanoeuvred its opponents on the Eastern Front for longer than any other tank. Deriving originally from the American Christie designs of the early 1930s, and more closely from the later Russian BT series, the T-34 went into production in 1940 and remained in service as the standard Russian medium tank throughout the war. The first main type was armed with a 76-mm gun, and this was gradually superseded from late 1943 by an up-gunned and up-armoured version mounting the 85-mm gun.

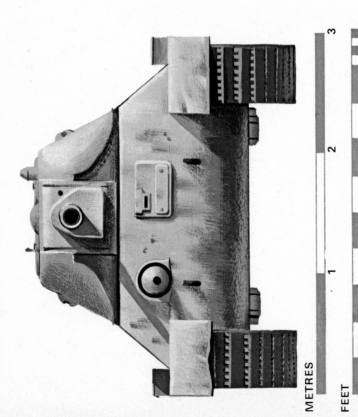

The T-34 was a robust and finely designed tank, combining to a high degree the essential qualities of firepower, mobility and protection. A predominant feature was the boldly sloped armour, which substantially reduced the penetrative power of enemy shells.

METRES
0   1   2   3

FEET
0   5   10

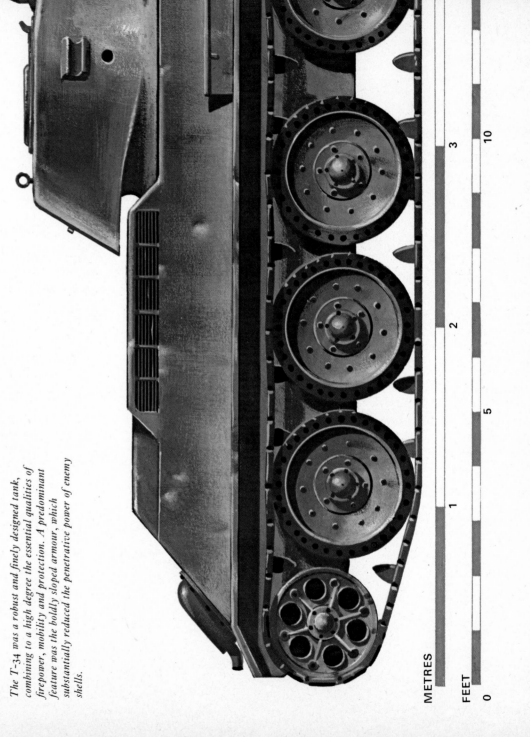

METRES
0   1   2   3

FEET
0   5   10

Once the crew was inside the tank, and the large turret hatch and the forward driver's hatch were shut, vision was limited to narrow episcopes let into the armour and to the commander's periscope mounted prominently on the turret. Normally, only the company commander's tank carried a radio. The T-34 ran on broad, 19-inch tracks and was able to keep going in soft conditions that often defeated its early German rivals, notably the Pzkw Marks III and IV.

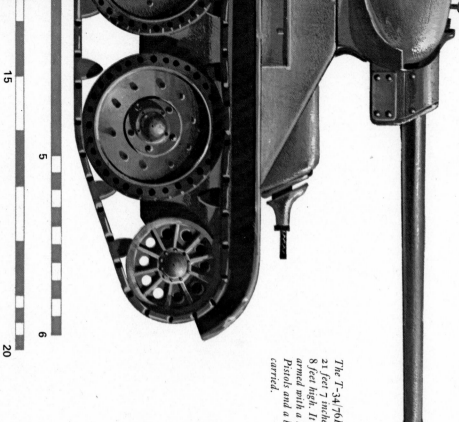

15
5
6
20

The T-34/76B shown here weighed 27¾ tons, it was 21 feet 7 inches long overall, 9 feet 10 inches wide and 8 feet high. It had a maximum speed of 32 mph and was armed with a long 76.2-mm gun and two machine-guns. Pistols and a box of hand grenades were usually also carried.

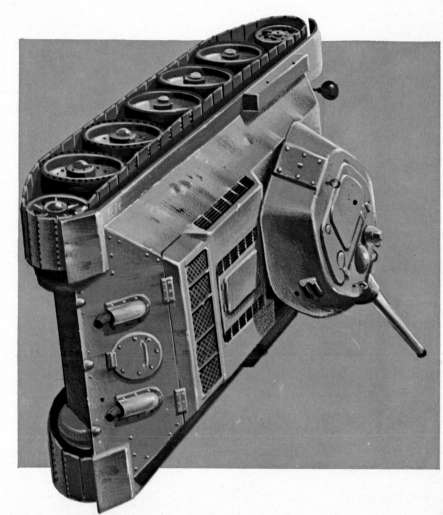

In previous campaigns the Luftwaffe had always provided invaluable air support for the Panzers, and in Russia it quickly achieved air superiority. Yet its operational efficiency was constantly impaired by the huge proportions of the land battle. This in turn laid a greater burden on the Panzers, and although they drove all before them in their great sweeping drives, Russian resistance from isolated pockets frustrated the eastward advance and bought time for Stalin to reorganize fresh armies for the defence of Moscow.

It will always be debated whether with a different strategy Hitler could have forced a decision in 1941. As it was he temporarily abandoned the drive to Moscow in August and concentrated on the Ukraine, where many Russian armies were encircled and destroyed; by September 1941 the German High Command estimated Russian losses at 2,500,000 men dead, wounded or taken prisoner, and 18,000 tanks and 14,000 aircraft destroyed.

When Hitler returned to the Moscow offensive in the early autumn it was too late: the rains came and choked the Panzer advance in a sea of mud just 40 miles west of the Russian capital. The Wehrmacht had carried out the greatest sustained offensive in military history but at a terrible cost; the infantry had lost 65% of its combat strength while the Panzers, in fighting tanks, were down to a third of their establishment. The forward elements were now being supplied on a hand-to-mouth basis and the Panzer leaders urged that Hitler allow them to adopt a flexible defence. But the German High Command was convinced that Russian resistance was at breaking-point and threw in its last reserves for a final effort.

The fighting in Russia was dominated at all times by the urgent needs of both sides for supplies of every kind on a massive scale. For the besieged and starving citizens of Leningrad (opposite) food as well as tanks was a top priority. During the first months of the Great Patriotic War some 1,500 industrial enterprises were evacuated to the east; shown above is a tank factory in the Urals, turning out T-34s. Meanwhile (below) the German High Command was directing more and more Panzers, like these Mark IV's, to the Eastern Front.

Heavy snow and sub-zero temperatures thwarted all their efforts and the advance staggered to a halt less than 20 miles from Moscow. Russian defences held; and then, in temperatures recording 40° of frost, the Russian field commander, Marshal Zhukov, hurled his Siberian divisions into a frantic counter-attack. Russian armour, now deployed in small battalion units,[2] hit the Germans hard while the Panzers lay immobilized through lack of winter oil. On 5 December Hitler ordered the Panzers to withdraw and refit while the infantry held the line, but as the Russian offensive gathered momentum it became impossible for the Panzers to disengage, and tanks and guns were abandoned in the chaos of retreat.

Hitler next took personal command of the front (by radio from Berlin) and turned his fury on his generals. Von Rundstedt, Guderian and Hoeppner (Fourth Panzer Group) joined the line of officers placed on the retired list for daring to give rather than hold ground. The Russians retained the initiative until the Germans were able to consolidate their defences in February 1942, and although Russian losses must have been enormous, Moscow was saved. The Panzers meanwhile had received their first serious defeat in their short but hitherto untarnished history.

THIS PAGE *German Mark III tanks (above) advance along snow-covered roads towards the Russian capital. When eventually the Germans were halted within 20 miles of Moscow Marshal Zhukov, commanding the city's defences, sent out specially equipped snow-troops with the armour (below) to beat back the enemy; the saving of Moscow marked the Panzers' first major defeat.*
OPPOSITE *A knocked-out Russian T-34 tank is left to burn.*

[2] A Russian tank brigade now consisted of two battalions each of 25 tanks.

Chapter Five

El Alamein to Victory

Throughout 1941, as the pace of the war quickened in Europe and the storm clouds gathered over the Pacific, the United States mobilized her industry for the mass production of munitions of war. Even at this stage American tanks were manifestly superior to those of Britain: they were manufactured from robust and well-tested components and were more suited to the rigours of combat than their more complex British counterparts.

The new American medium tank was the Lee-Grant (Medium M-3); it went into quantity production in July 1941 and more than 2,000 were produced in the first six months. The Lee version was produced first and the Grant followed shortly afterwards; the two were broadly similar except that the Grant mounted the square-shaped, British-style turret. Although they were mechanically sound and adequately protected with welded armour, nevertheless their ungainly layout resulted in major tactical disadvantages, for in most positions the tank had to be turned on its tracks before the side-mounted 75-mm gun could fire. The Medium M-3 was intended to fill the void until a more battleworthy medium tank with a turret-mounted 75-mm gun could be produced. This requirement was met in the spring of 1942 by the Sherman, or M-4. Constructed of cast armour and equipped with a high-

velocity gun, the Sherman gave the Allies a tank which at last allowed them to engage the Panzers on a more equal footing. The Sherman was fast and highly manoeuvrable even though, like the Grant, it suffered tactically because it was powered by bulky radial engines which made for a high silhouette. Its components were strong on simplicity and ruggedness: features of particular interest were the volute-spring, bogie-type suspension – which gave improved mobility and effectiveness over rough terrain – the highly-developed V-8 engine and the rubber-block, rubber-jointed tracks. A life of 3,000 miles was not unusual for these tracks, compared for example to about 600 miles for the metal-jointed tracks on the Panzer Mark IV. Altogether 49,234 Shermans were produced, and the large numbers supplied to the Allied armies now made possible the massing of superior tank forces in critical areas, while their speed and capacity for sustained operation under severe conditions made them a vital factor in the Allied victory.

Initially most of the new American tanks were despatched to the Western Desert to re-equip British armoured divisions, which by the summer of 1942 were in a desperate plight. A continued adherence to dated cavalry tactics was still resulting in enormous casualties at the hands of Rommel and the Panzer Mark IV; while the British infantry had lost the last shreds of any faith in the protective powers of its armoured divisions. Thus a situation close to 'apartheid' had grown up between the two arms.

OPPOSITE *The barrel of a Grant tank's 75-mm gun gets a pull-through. Though awkwardly mounted in a side sponson, this gun lent much-needed weight to the Allied forces in North Africa.*
THIS PAGE *Once in enemy hands tanks were subjected to much scrutiny and were also remanned and used against the original owners, like this captured Matilda (above); note the spaced turret armour. Below is a knocked-out German Mark III.*

THE ALLIED SHERMANS

The Sherman was the standard Allied medium tank from 1943. As the Lee-Grant's successor it made use of many of the latter's components but its fighting capabilities were much improved by mounting the 75-mm gun in a turret with all-round traverse. The gun, moreover, was hydro-electrically stabilized, which meant that aimed fire could be achieved while the tank was on the move. This was a new development but it was not without its drawbacks in the early years.

Introduced in time to join the Eighth Army at El Alamein, the Sherman was then produced in great numbers and at high speed. Altogether 49,234 were built by Ford, Chrysler, General Motors and other enterprises in some twenty different marks. At the peak of its production a finished Sherman could be assembled from prefabricated parts in 30 minutes.

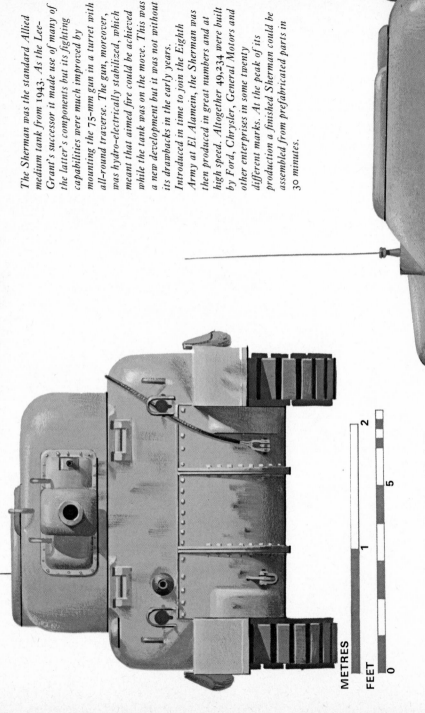

METRES

FEET

ABOVE AND BELOW The 30.2-ton M-4 A-1 (Mark II) Sherman shown here from front and side in its desert livery was 19 feet 7 inches long, 8 feet 9 inches wide and 9 feet 2 inches high. It had rubber block tracks and a maximum speed of 25 mph. It was armed with the 75-mm gun and three machine-guns.

METRES

FEET

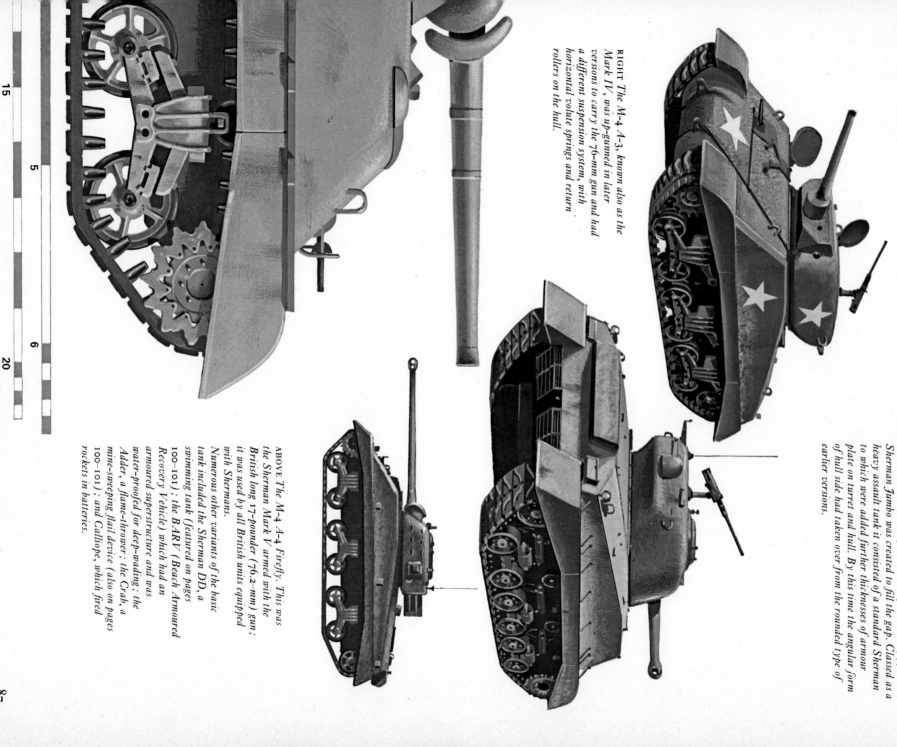

RIGHT *The M-4-A-3, known also as the Mark IV, was up-gunned in later versions to carry the 76-mm gun and had a different suspension system, with horizontal volute springs and return rollers on the hull.*

LEFT *In the absence of a US heavy tank in 1944 the Sherman Jumbo was created to fill the gap. Classed as a heavy assault tank it consisted of a standard Sherman to which were added further thicknesses of armour plate on turret and hull. By this time the angular form of hull side had taken over from the rounded type of earlier versions.*

ABOVE *The M-4-A-4 Firefly. This was the Sherman Mark V armed with the British long 17-pounder (76.2-mm) gun; it was used by all British units equipped with Shermans.*
Numerous other variants of the basic tank included the Sherman DD, a swimming tank (featured on pages 100–101); the BARV (Beach Armoured Recovery Vehicle) which had an armoured superstructure and was water-proofed for deep-wading; the Adder, a flame-thrower; the Crab, a mine-sweeping flail device (also on pages 100–101); and Calliope, which fired rockets in batteries.

Rommel's supply position had in the meantime deteriorated but nevertheless by August 1942 he had penetrated deep into Egypt and had pinned the British at El Alamein. Now the Afrika Korps gathered its resources and prepared for the final push for the Suez Canal. Fortunately for the Allies, at this precise moment a commander arrived for the Eighth Army who, though new to desert warfare, was not in the least overawed by the myth of Rommel. By making a few changes to the defence plans of his predecessor, Auchinleck, General Montgomery deployed his new American Grants in hull-down positions along the Alam Halfa ridge; the infantry was secure behind the protection of deep minefields and there was ample artillery support. As the Panzer spearheads wilted before the British defences the Royal Air Force roamed freely in the skies above, raining destruction and chaos on the vulnerable Axis supply lines. After a week of bloody fighting Rommel admitted failure and withdrew his battered formations behind their defences to the west of El Alamein. Montgomery waited six weeks before launching his great offensive against the Afrika Korps. The Battle of El Alamein (23 October – 4 November 1942), with its secure flanks and massive concentrations of infantry and artillery, was closer in character to the Battle of the Somme than any previous desert encounter. Sherman tanks arrived in the theatre in time for British brigades to be equipped with them for the battle; but although he possessed an enormous

superiority in tanks, in the event Montgomery allocated the armour a secondary, non-cavalry role.

After the British had broken through the German defences and won the infantry dog-fight, Montgomery mounted a cautious and closely-controlled pursuit of the Afrika Korps. Many historians have since criticized his handling of the armour in the pursuit, for indeed, with fewer than 40 combat tanks by that stage, the Germans could have done little to prevent a bold Allied move. However, Montgomery held firmly to his conviction that he had already defeated the Afrika Korps at El Alamein, and consequently there was no need to take extra risks. Although British tank tactics lacked glamour, Montgomery managed to teach Rommel and the Panzers what the French should have taught them in 1940, namely that the tank is a brittle weapon of war. The tank in fact met its true fate in the Western Desert – from the air. The reason for this is that armour needs an elaborate supply and logistical structure which is vulnerable to disruptive air attacks unless a defending air force can produce an umbrella; and in the Western Desert no such umbrella was available to Rommel and his armour.

Nevertheless the Desert War dragged on for another six months, and although the Torch Landings in French North Africa in November 1942 sealed the fate of the Afrika Korps, the Panzers were still able to demonstrate new skills in the use of tanks in the defence. In the end,

OPPOSITE *Shermans at El Alamein, seen moving up (above), re-stocking with ammunition (below left) and being carried on a 'portee' transporter (below right).*
ABOVE *A halted German tank crew bows to British bayonets.*
BELOW *British infantrymen take cover behind an abandoned enemy tank.*

however, neither side learned the right lessons; each saw the desert as a specialized theatre of warfare from which it was impossible to draw conclusions. Each, furthermore, still believed in the idea of an all-powerful armoured torrent, but it was the Germans who were to make the fatal errors. They did so at Stalingrad, soon after the defeat at El Alamein, and later at Kursk in the summer of 1943.

The Eastern Front

On the Eastern Front the Panzers spearheaded the great spring offensive of 1942 towards Stalingrad and the Volga. In the main they were equipped at this time with the excellent Mark IV tank which, if it possessed none of the skilfully sloped armour of the T-34, was capable of meeting its opponents on equal terms because of the expertise of the Panzer crews and the hitting power of the high-velocity 75-mm cannon. This tank was destined to give the Panzer divisions good service right up to the end of the war; even so Hitler and his generals had already become obsessed with the need to reassert the technical superiority of their tanks over the Russians. Combat officers at the front, in a counsel of despair, advocated the production of T-34s for their own use since they believed it could not be bettered. But German industry could never have coped with the technicalities of such a project – even if such a decision had been politically acceptable, which it clearly was not.

Instead the High Command flirted with numerous designs for heavy tanks and super-monsters, which wasted valuable industrial capacity while the Panzers at the front had to make do with the Mark III, the Mark IV and indifferent assault guns. Eventually two prototypes went into quantity production: known as the Tiger and the Panther, these tanks were destined to play a major part in Panzer fortunes in the final period of the war. The Tiger weighed 56 tons, had a maximum of 100 mm of frontal armour and was armed with the excellent 88-mm gun; it put the Germans ahead of the Russians and well in advance of the Anglo-Americans. All the same the Tiger had more

than its share of teething problems but the Germans, instead of patiently solving these first, rushed the tank into a premature deployment. It received its baptism of fire in a secondary operation, in unsuitable terrain on the Leningrad Front in September 1942, where the Russians inflicted heavy casualties and the decisive factor of surprise was destroyed. Meanwhile the Panther's designers ran into even greater technical problems in the initial period of that tank's construction, and the delay incurred before it was finally considered ready for combat was to have a major influence on the course of events in 1943.

In the autumn of 1942 the German offensive was forced to a halt, trapped in the claustrophobic arena of Stalingrad – where the Wehrmacht was destined to suffer its greatest single defeat of World War II. The concepts of Blitzkrieg were totally irrelevant in Stalingrad. There the Panzers forfeited all the advantages of their mobile tactics and allowed the Russian infantry to dictate the mode of combat. Marshal Zhukov, the Russian commander, contained the Germans in the city and in November unleashed his new tank armies in a massive counter-attack against indifferent satellite armies fighting on the German flanks. The Russian pincer linked up at Kalatsch on the Don, trapping von Paulus and the 20 divisions that composed his Sixth Army. Hitler refused permission for von Paulus to break out from Stalingrad and instead, in Operation Winter Storm, launched Hoth and the Fourth Panzer Army in a vain attempt to effect a relief. On 2 February 1943 the pathetic remains of the Sixth Army surrendered.

OPPOSITE *German infantrymen stick close to the cover of their tanks in the steady advance across the Russian steppes during the spring offensive of 1942.*

ABOVE *A Russian shell bursts ahead of a Mark IV pressing with infantry support through a maize field in the same campaign, directed towards Stalingrad and the Volga.*

BELOW *A German Mark III tank fords a river in Russia. The vast spaces to be covered on the Eastern Front took a heavy toll of German equipment.*

semi-fixed positions. Moreover production on a large scale inevitably absorbed part of the German industrial capacity which could otherwise have been devoted to tanks.[1]

After Stalingrad the Soviet tank armies found new strength and vigour. Work began on developing the excellent and by no means obsolescent T-34 to mount the 85-mm high-velocity gun in place of the 76-mm version. Substantial American aid in the form of vehicles and canned foods revolutionized Soviet supply problems and allowed the tank divisions to attempt new dimensions in penetrative power. The Russian generals had learned the lessons of the past and now handled their tank formations with confidence and skill. Their weakness lay in their tendency to continue offensives which were unprofitable and resulted in disproportionately heavy casualties. It was this willingness on the part of the Russians to be lavish with their human material, of which they had a great abundance, together with the technical excellence of the Wehrmacht in the defence, that allowed the front to be stabilized and gave the Panzers a chance to recover from the disasters of Stalingrad. In March 1943 von Manstein and his Army Group South recaptured Kharkov in a brilliant armoured operation in which the Tigers were able to demonstrate for the first time their true potential.

Hitler had earlier recalled Germany's greatest tank soldier, Heinz Guderian, from an obscure retirement, and offered him the post of Inspector-General of Armoured Troops. He was given the equivalent powers of an army commander and had control over all Panzer and motorized troops, though not of the artillery Jagdpanzers. The stable front in Russia now attracted Hitler and his closest advisers to the possibilities of securing a decision through a bold use of armour. But Guderian, together with General Model (then commanding the Ninth Army) counselled against any new offensives, saying that the Panzer divisions were in desperate need of a major rest and refit. Guderian had detected a disturbing inflationary situation in his new command, for while the number of divisions had been increased the tank complement per division had shrunk. After much debate Hitler ignored Guderian's and Model's advice in favour of launching a massive tank offensive against the Russian salient around Kursk. Events moved swiftly toward what General von Mellenthin (at that time Chief of Staff to 56th Panzer Corps) was to describe as the *Todesritt*, or death ride, of the Panzers:

The German Army threw away all its advantages in mobile war and met the Russians on ground of their own choosing.... the German High Command could think of nothing better to do than fling our magnificent Panzers against the strongest fortress in the world.
From *Panzer Battles*, by General F. W. von Mellenthin

[1] In October 1942 the monthly production figures for the Mark IV reached the modest total of 100. The highest annual figure in Germany was that for 1944, when 19,000 armoured vehicles were built; in the same period the British produced 30,000, the Russians 30,000, and the Americans 90,000.

Besides the enormous losses in manpower the Germans lost 60,000 vehicles and 1,500 tanks – figures that represent the equivalent of six months' production. The shock to the German Army was immense, and it was a blow from which the élite Panzer formations never recovered. The average tank complement in a Panzer division on the Eastern Front was now down to 27 tanks and the only proven vehicle the Germans had was the Mark IV. Behind the front German tank policy was in confusion: the new designs were still nowhere near ready while the artillery wanted the High Command to concentrate on producing a new tank destroyer to replace the vulnerable towed anti-tank gun.

The new weapon, called the Jagdpanzer, was a high-velocity 75-mm gun mounted on a tank chassis. Its form in fact symbolized the change which had come over German thinking about Panzers. For the Jagdpanzer was essentially a *defensive* weapon, best used for ambushes or in

OPPOSITE Two new German tanks which made indifferent debuts on the Eastern Front but which were later to guide the fortunes of the Panzers were the Mark VI Tiger (top) and (centre) the Mark V Panther. In the bottom picture von Kleist's tanks are seen crossing the Don.

ABOVE A German Mark IV is silhouetted against the smoke from the fighting around Stalingrad.

BELOW Russian infantrymen race forward behind their armour at Kalatsch, where the Russians closed a critical pincer on the trapped German Sixth Army; the survivors surrendered in February 1943.

The offensive at Kursk was delayed until July 1943 because the new Panthers were not available in sufficient quantity (there were only 100 on the Eastern Front in April) and in the meantime the whole plan of operations had been compromised by the Lucy Ring – an OSS espionage service based in Switzerland. The Russians planned accordingly and met the Panzer thrusts with a seemingly impregnable network of defences. Rokossovsky's Army, for example, which was deployed to resist the northern thrust by Model's Ninth Army, had prepared 3,000 miles of trenches and 400,000 mines, i.e. 2,400 anti-tank and 2,700 anti-personnel mines per mile of front; on average there were 150 guns and mortars per mile of front. Amidst the maze of trenches and minefields the main Russian stratagem centred on the 'Pak-fronts', which involved groups of 10 anti-tank guns capable of providing concentrated fire through a centralized command. Once the German advance had been blunted on these defences Zhukov planned to unleash Koniev's central reserve force with its tank armies in a massive counter-offensive.

Hitler was gambling for high stakes at Kursk since the 78 Panzer and Panzer Grenadier divisions deployed there represented nearly all his armour and more than half the line formations available to him on the Eastern Front. However, there could be few less rewarding ways to deploy tanks than at this 'Panzer Verdun'. The basic formation was the Panzer *Keil*, or wedge, a battering-ram technique the spearhead of which was composed of Tigers and lumbering Ferdinands, with the lighter Mark IVs and Panthers deployed on the flanks and mechanized infantry bringing up the rear. The Ferdinands, encountered here for the first time and also known as the Porsche Tiger or 'Elefant', was an enormous self-propelled gun. It weighed 65 tons, had a crew of six, was armed with the 88-mm L-70 gun but had no machine-guns for self-defence. Its frontal armour was 8 inches thick, i.e. more than the British battlecruisers at Jutland in 1916; its top speed was 12 mph and it needed another Ferdinand or Tiger to recover it when it broke down.

The battle began on 4 July 1943, bringing into collision the greatest single assembly of armoured vehicles in military history. The Panzer *Keil* proved to be an immediate failure as the Russians separated the infantry from the armour, peeled away the weaker tanks on the flanks and exposed the heavy Tigers and Ferdinands to overwhelming concentrations of fire. The Panthers, too, did not come up to expectations: they were easily set ablaze because their oil and gasoline feeding systems were inadequately protected, and the crews were insufficiently trained.

The application of Russian bulk against German skill slowed the advance right down and by 12 July it had stalled in the crippling grasp of the minefields. Model in the north had made no headway against Rokossovsky while Hoth in the south after enormous losses had penetrated 20 miles in nine days – a far cry from the heady days of 1940. On 13 July the Fourth Panzer Army had 600 tanks remaining and these Hoth hurled forward in one last desperate attempt to break through; the 'death ride' had begun. Zhukov's Fifth Tank Army blocked the way and 1,500 tanks clashed in close-quarter combat; then, at ranges of often less than 100 yards, the T-34s pressed home the battle. In one day the Wehrmacht lost 400 tanks and more than 10,000 men and the Panzer divisions never recovered from these losses. Zhukov now moved over to a major offensive and pushed the shattered Panzers back beyond Kharkov and the Soviet western frontiers.

SOVIET ARMOURED FORMATIONS

By the end of 1942 Soviet tank brigades were being combined into larger formations. Varying combinations of the four categories shown below were used to make up the tank armies.

1 TANK CORPS

This varied in size but at its maximum consisted of the following units:

CORPS HEADQUARTERS

- 1 motorcycle battalion
- 1 recce battalion
- 2 heavy tank battalions
- 3 tank brigades
- 1 motorized infantry brigade
- 1 support brigade

Total Corps strength: 300 tanks (similar to a Panzer division).

2 MECHANIZED CORPS

This was similar in organization to a Panzer Grenadier Division:

CORPS HEADQUARTERS

- 3 motorized infantry brigades
- 3 tank battalions
- 1 tank brigade
- 2 self-propelled gun regiments
- 2 anti-tank regiments
- 1 rocket regiment
- 1 mortar regiment
- support elements

3 INDEPENDENT TANK BRIGADE

Each brigade had 107 T-34 tanks plus support elements.

4 HEAVY TANK REGIMENT

In the early stages this had 23 KV-1 tanks; later it was equipped with JS-IIs and JS-IIIs.

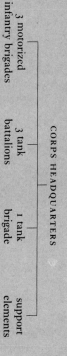

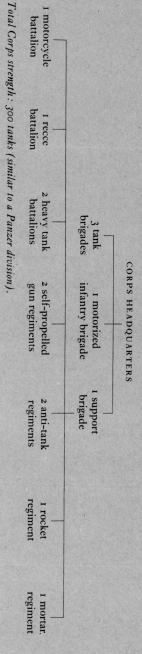

OPPOSITE *German tanks and armoured cars regroup before a blazing skyline.* RIGHT *Russian soldiers at Kursk (above) examine two knocked-out German Ferdinands, the ponderous self-propelled guns which by their lack of mobility — and machine-guns — were easily isolated and destroyed. In the lower picture a Panzer grenadier dashes round two immobilized Russian vehicles, a heavy BA-32 armoured car fitted with a 45-mm tank gun, and a KV-11, the monster tank which mounted a 152-mm howitzer.*

ABOVE *The Allied invasion of Europe began with the assault on what Churchill thought was the enemy's 'soft underbelly', namely Italy. Here a Sherman disembarks from its landing craft.*

BELOW *Shermans head north after a bitter winter campaign; far from being a straightforward push, it took the Allies 11 months to reach Rome after the first landings in Sicily.*

OPPOSITE *Rehearsals (above) for the Normandy landings feature an AVRE, capable of bridging a 30-foot gap. In the lower picture are lines of Normandy-bound Shermans parked 'somewhere in England'.*

The Invasion of Europe

The Battle of Kursk was both an admission that armour had become fatally inhibited by its enemies on the ground and in the air. Hitler, however, still believed that his armour was a battle-winning force, and as the Western Allies began their invasion of Europe — from the Mediterranean in 1943 and Normandy in 1944 — he sought to use his tanks to exploit imagined schisms in the Western Alliance. German defences in the west were based on a compromise between the fortifications of the Atlantic Wall and the mobile reserves of Panzer Group West, whose better divisions were concentrated to meet what was considered to be the likely Allied avenue of advance through the Pas de Calais.

Rommel was given the task of countering the Allied invasion and his planning was hopelessly wrong. He envisaged the Allied landings as an infantry assault that would create a beachhead into which Allied armour would be deployed. Consequently he moved his tanks close to the coast so that they could destroy the beachheads before the Allied tanks were ashore. But, unfortunately for Rommel, the Allies had developed specialized amphibious and assault armour which moved in with the infantry: these were the tanks of Major-General Hobart's 79th Division, developed from Sherman, Valentine and Churchill chassis. Popularly known as the 'Funnies', they stormed ashore in one of the most brilliant armoured operations of World War II.

These special vehicles included the Sherman DD (Duplex Drive) amphibious tank; the Crab — a flail tank for exploding mines; the Churchill Ark and AVRE, which were gap-crossing combat vehicles, and the Crocodile, which was a flame-thrower. Their contributions to the British landings were invaluable while their absence (except for the Sherman DD) on the American beaches resulted in heavy casualties on D-Day (6 June 1944).

Once they were ashore the Allies' problems centred around the need to break out of the Bocage, where the wooded terrain favoured the defence and inhibited Allied armour. In this close country the Jagdpanzer and the Tiger were supreme; there was no Allied equivalent to these giants for the simple reason that the requirements of sea transport limited tank weights at that time to a maximum of 40 tons, and consequently the Allies had been unable to develop their own heavy battle tanks. The Americans still relied upon Shermans while the British had developed some of their Shermans to mount the new 17-pounder anti-tank gun — the product being known as the Sherman Firefly. But other British tanks such as the infantry Churchill were of little value, in the latter's case because its lack of speed was not compensated for either by extra protection or increased firepower. The latest tank of the cruiser lineage, the Cromwell, also made its début at this time: it had a strange, square turret and though fast and tactically mobile it was no match for the Tigers and Panthers.

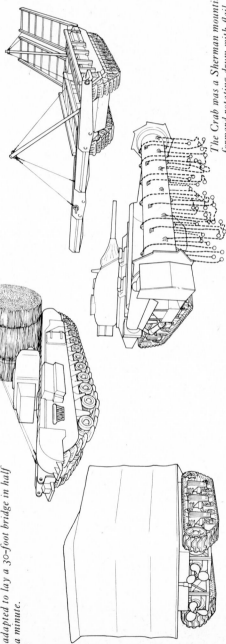

The AVRE (Armoured Vehicle Royal Engineer), here carrying a fascine for ditch-crossing work, could also be adapted to lay a 30-foot bridge in half a minute.

The Ark was a gap-crossing vehicle consisting of a Churchill hull with ramps fitted to front and rear.

The Crab was a Sherman mounting a forward rotating drum with flail attachments that exploded a path through the minefields on the landing beaches.

The Sherman DD (Duplex Drive) was an amphibious vehicle kept buoyant by its all-round folding canvas screen and driven through the water by its two propellers.

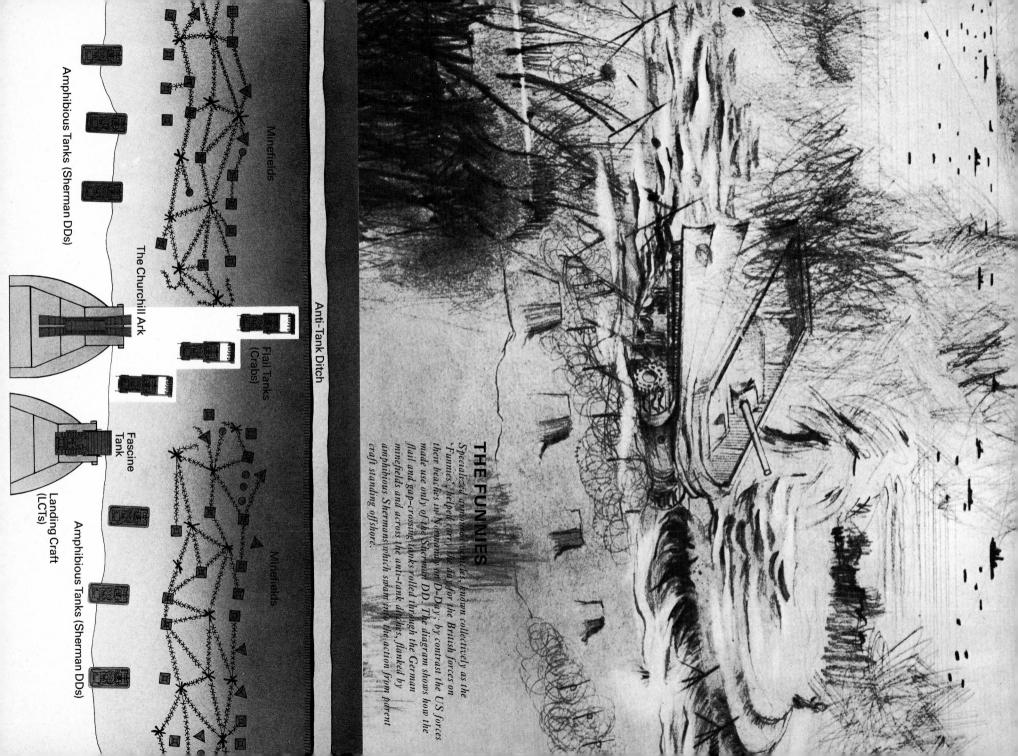

THE FUNNIES

Specialized armoured vehicles, known collectively as the 'Funnies', helped carry the day for the British forces on their beaches in Normandy on D-Day; by contrast the US forces made use only of the Sherman DD. The diagram shows how the flail and gap-crossing tanks rolled through the German minefields and across the anti-tank ditches, flanked by amphibious Shermans which swam into the action from parent craft standing offshore.

Amphibious Tanks (Sherman DDs)

Minefields

The Churchill Ark

Flail Tanks
(Crabs)

Anti-Tank Ditch

Fascine
Tank

Landing Craft
(LCTs)

Amphibious Tanks (Sherman DDs)

Minefields

For both sides morale was a major factor in the ensuing tank encounters that occurred in Western Europe. The Allies recognized that in order to destroy a Tiger or a Panther they would have to lose a number of tanks before the superior German vehicle could be taken in the flank. Conversely the Panzers fought their tanks in the knowledge

that no matter how many Cromwells or Shermans exploded under their fire, eventually they would be overcome by sheer force of numbers. The major advantage for the Allies lay in their total air superiority, while for the Panzers the sky became a source of terror and manoeuvre in daylight was tantamount to suicide. In the Battle of the Bocage, Allied armoured tactics proved suspect and Montgomery learned the hard way – through such costly failures as Operation Goodwood – that material superiority can be neutralized by local conditions. As the British tanks tried to bludgeon a path through to Caen and the open country beyond, German tanks and assault guns, mines and Panzerfausts (infantry rocket launchers) took a fearful toll. While the British and the Germans were locked in their deadly combat for Caen General Bradley, commanding the US 12th Army Group, deployed General Patton and his

Third Army for the breakout at St Lô. Operation Cobra, as it was called, hit the Wehrmacht when its High Command was still reeling from the shock of the abortive plot against Hitler, and those divisions that stood their ground were engulfed in a hailstorm of fire as Patton broke free of the Bocage. American armour and infantry divisions moved west into Brittany, south to the Loire and then east toward the strategic centre of Le Mans. The British and Canadians took Caen and moved south towards Falaise, trapping the Wehrmacht in a rapidly closing pincer. The Allied formations packed the shoulders of the pocket and destroyed 19 German divisions with artillery and air bombardment. Patton wanted to close the gap with his Shermans but Bradley wisely decided that the Allied tanks would be unable to prevent the Panzers from breaking out. Those Germans who did manage to escape had eventually to swim for their lives across the Seine, and 2,000 tanks and assault guns were either captured or destroyed.

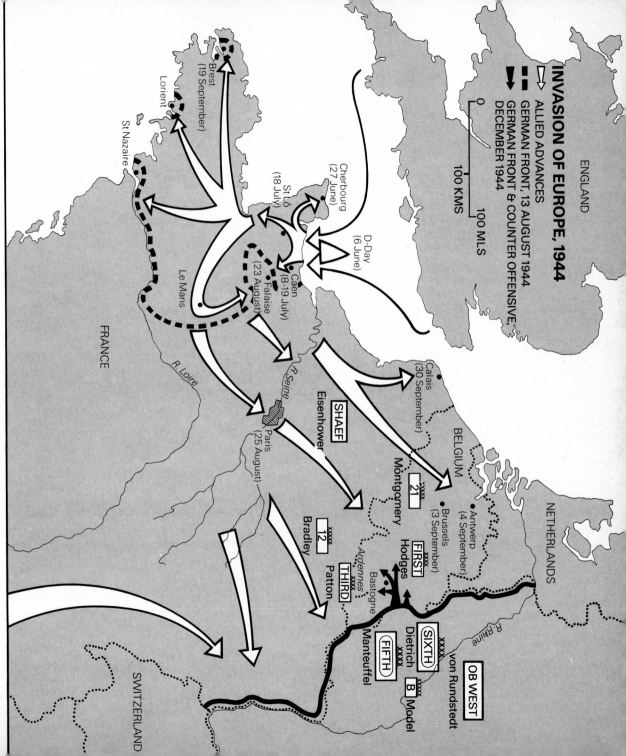

ALLIED ADVANCES
GERMAN FRONT, 13 AUGUST 1944
GERMAN FRONT & COUNTER OFFENSIVE, DECEMBER 1944

0   100 KMS
0   100 MLS

ENGLAND

Brest (19 September)
Lorient
St Nazaire
Cherbourg (27 June)
St Lô (18 July)
D-Day (6 June)
Caen (8–19 July)
Falaise (23 August)
Le Mans
Paris (25 August)
R. Loire
R. Seine
Calais (30 September)
Antwerp (4 September)
Brussels (3 September)
BELGIUM
NETHERLANDS
FRANCE
SWITZERLAND

SHAEF
Eisenhower

21 xxxx
Montgomery

12 xxxx
Bradley

FIRST xxxx
Hodges

THIRD xxxx
Patton

Ardennes
Bastogne

SIXTH xxxx
Dietrich

FIFTH xxxx
Manteuffel

B xxxx
Model

OB WEST
von Rundstedt

R. Rhine

As the Allies swept across France and Belgium in late 1944, and slogged their way more slowly up through Italy, the German armour was increasingly forced onto the defensive. In the upper picture is a Tiger at Bastogne; below is a Mark IV backed into an outbuilding to serve as an anti-tank gun.

OPPOSITE Tanks link up with airborne assault forces beside a glider landing ground. Below is an Allied tank fitted with a rocket-launcher attachment.

Now 20 divisions of Allied armour spearheaded the pursuit of the retreating Wehrmacht through eastern France and the Low Countries to the western frontier of the Third Reich. An armoured division took up 200 miles of road and the logistical problems were intensified as the supply lines became longer and longer, stretching back to their base ports at Cherbourg and Marseilles (liberated on 28 August). To maintain a controlled advance Eisenhower insisted on adhering to a basic linear strategy – with all armies keeping pace with those on their flanks – though he did sanction Montgomery's attempt in September to secure the bridges over the Waal, Maas and the Rhine through the use of airborne formations. The first and second bridges were taken intact but Allied armour failed to effect a relief of the British airborne troops at Arnhem.

By October 1944 the Allies had 70 divisions spread out over 500 miles of front but they were still a long way short of the autumn objective – the Rhine. Despite Montgomery's capture of Antwerp, the Germans still held the Scheldt estuary, with the result that the Allies lacked a major port east of Cherbourg; this, coupled with the early onset of winter and a general exhaustion, resulted in the Allied advance losing momentum just as German resistance stiffened along the western frontiers.

Hitler then attempted one last Panzer gamble. In December he hurled his remaining tanks in a desperate and foolhardy counter-offensive through the Ardennes. The famous Battle of the Bulge which resulted was an attempt to drive a wedge politically and militarily between the British and Americans by recapturing Antwerp. The assault by the Sixth SS Panzer Army and the Fifth Panzer

Army caught the Americans by surprise, and with Allied aircraft grounded by bad weather the Germans at first drove all before them. But the Allied reaction after the initial shock was rapid and decisive. An airborne division held out in Bastogne while the infantry divisions packed the flanks of the breakthrough and denied the vital crossings over the Meuse. Patton moved quickly in a bold drive with his tanks through the Upper Ardennes to relieve Bastogne. On Christmas Eve 1944 the weather cleared and 5,000 tactical aircraft took to the skies and rained havoc and destruction on the exposed Panzers and their supply formations. The German offensive was contained, the Allies regrouped and launched a massive counter-offensive which moved slowly forward through the winter months and so reached the Rhine.

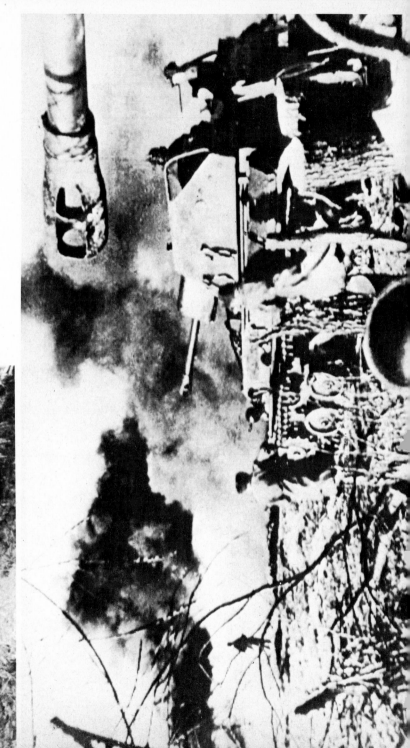

Balance of Forces FINAL RUSSIAN OFFENSIVE 16 APRIL - 7 MAY 1945		
CATEGORY	RUSSIA	GERMANY
Divisions	193	85
Men	2,500,000	1,000,000
Guns/mortars	41,000	10,000
Tanks/self-propelled guns	6,250	1,500
Aircraft	7,500	3,300

LEFT *A Panzer grenadier on the Eastern Front waits for further orders in the shelter of a tank.*
BELOW *Waves of Red Army infantry charge German-held positions.*
OPPOSITE *Russian infantry (above) ride across a stream on a detachment of T-34/85s. Below, a parade of JS IIIs, the latest Russian battle tank of the war; mounting a mighty 122-mm gun, JS IIIs took part in the final assault on Berlin.*

The Fall of Berlin

In their last great offensive of the war the Panzers had bought the Third Reich a few extra weeks of life in the west and had inflicted on the Americans their biggest single defeat in the European war. But the price they paid for this defiant gesture was soon to be felt on the Eastern Front, where, as the Russian army groups deployed along the Oder for the last offensive into Berlin, precious few tanks remained to oppose them. At dawn on 16 April 1945 40,000 guns opened fire on a 250-mile front and 6,000 Soviet tanks began to move along the last 50 miles of road into Berlin. The bulk of the Russian armour consisted of well-tried T-34s supplemented by small numbers of the latest battle tanks, which arrived in time for the final battle. The new tank, the JS III, had been developed from the KV series and its sloping armour and 122-mm gun gave it a powerful battle capability; but firepower and protection had been compromised and it could carry only small reserves of ammunition.

The final march on Berlin was not, as it has often been presented, an impressive armoured punch: indeed the tanks found little freedom to move against the German defences. The Wehrmacht and SS Divisions fought with enormous devotion to a lost cause, no quarter was asked or given and casualties were enormous on both sides. When the Russians eventually encircled Berlin they hurled their tanks with optimistic arrogance into the street battles only to see them destroyed piecemeal by fanatical defenders equipped with the short-range but lethal Panzerfaust.

On 25 April the last barrage of the war on the Eastern Front began as 2,000,000 shells rained down on to the inner suburbs of Berlin. Soviet infantry and armour fought its way forward from street to street until only a few acres round the Reich Chancellery and Hitler's bunker survived. On 30 April, Hitler committed suicide and General Krebs, Chief of Staff of the 56th Panzer Corps, surrendered the remnants of the Berlin garrison to General Vasili Chuikov, commander of the Eighth Guards Army, and the battle was over.

While the battle for Berlin was being fought, Allied armour in the west had crossed the Rhine and moved eastwards to link up with the Russians on the Elbe. Patton and the Third Army swung south into Austria while Montgomery and the British sped across the old Panzer training areas on the Lüneburg Heath to Hamburg. Two new Allied tanks appeared in time to join the final phase of the fighting and these helped somewhat to restore the prestige of Allied armour. The Americans had the Pershing, an excellent tank armed with a 90-mm gun, while the British had the Comet, which exploited the mechanical reliability of the Cromwell and had a new 75-mm gun and sloped armour – factors which combined to make it, belatedly, the best British tank of the war.

OPPOSITE The combined assault from east and west on Germany's last strongholds. *Above*, Russian armour enters Berlin. *Below*, Pershing tanks of the US Ninth Army cross the Rhine under strong air cover.

THIS PAGE A new British cruiser tank which entered service shortly before the end of the war was the Comet (*above*). This was a much improved version of the Cromwell (*below*), which had been introduced in the previous year.

Tanks in the Far East and Pacific

In the period up to the end of World War II the tank made its most spectacular contributions to the battlefield in the Western world. Yet this account would certainly be incomplete if mention were not made of the role of the tank in the Far East and generally in the war against Japan.

There were only a few isolated instances of tank battles as such, and this was because the Japanese had earlier paid scant attention to the tank; consequently those which they did possess were decidedly inferior to Western types. In these circumstances the Allied tank crews found themselves acting mainly in the role of self-propelled artillery in close support of the infantry. In Burma, the Pacific atolls and New Guinea the tanks engaged Japanese pill-boxes and strongpoints at close range and in terrain where air support and conventional, i.e. static, artillery proved less effective.

At first the enormous logistical problems involved made the Allied use lighter tanks than were best suited to these theatres of operation, but the need was soon appreciated for more powerful, better protected and more heavily armed cruiser tanks. In the Pacific this placed a new premium on landing ships and assault craft, while in Burma it required feats of engineering wizardry before the primitive hill roads and jungle trails could support the weight of Grants and Shermans.

The British had the additional problem of training units of their redoubtable Indian soldiery in the technological skills needed to man and maintain sophisticated armour in battle. But all the time, effort and sweat that went into the creation and deployment of an Indian Armoured Corps quickly paid dividends. In the seemingly impenetrable jungle the Shermans hurled aside natural obstacles and paved a way to the very mouths of the Japanese bunkers in operations which added fresh scope to the concept of mobile fire support.

This story was repeated on innumerable occasions in the Pacific, where the tanks were present from the first offensive at Guadalcanal (1942–43) to the final amphibious operation at Okinawa in 1945. The Pacific campaign is also important in the present context because of its contribution to the development of amphibious armoured operations. Specialized vehicles known as Landing Vehicles Tracked (LVTs) were originally developed by the US Marine Corps in 1940 as unarmoured supply carriers. Then on Tarawa in 1943 they were employed as armoured assault carriers; these were later joined by turreted gun-carrying versions. Eight Marine and Army LVT battalions led the amphibious assault on Saipan in June 1944 and by the end of the war the Marine Corps alone had 12 LVT battalions deployed in the Pacific theatre.

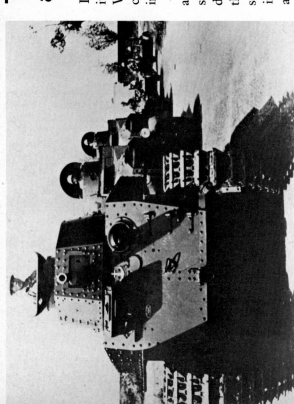

ABOVE *Two Japanese tanks which served in the Malayan and Pacific campaigns, the light type 95 (top) and the medium Type 97 (centre).*
BELOW *American Shermans at a river crossing in Luzon in June 1945.*

TOP British tanks manned by the Indian Armoured Corps move up for the final assault on Fort Dufferin, Mandalay, in March 1945.
CENTRE A US flamethrower fires on a Japanese strongpoint in the Philippines.
RIGHT A Landing Vehicle Tracked (LVT); the importance of these specialized US vehicles grew with the increase in amphibious assault work.

The danger in studying the history and performance of a weapon system in isolation is that its contribution on the battlefield may be exaggerated. The history of the tank is one of an attempt to transform a siege-breaking machine into the armoured horse of mechanized cavalry. The late Sir Basil Liddell-Hart contended, along with other writers of military history, that ever since the Napoleonic era the weapons of the defence have gained a growing material superiority over those of the offence. Certainly the tank never became the invincible armoured horse; and its one phase of superiority, achieved by Guderian and his Panzers in 1940, was in essence an aberration caused by the French High Command's crass neglect of the principles of defence in battle.

In the decisive battles of World War II – Stalingrad, El Alamein, and the D-Day Landings – the tank was not the decisive or even the predominant weapon. Kursk, though rightly claimed as the greatest tank encounter in history, was a massive battle of attrition nearer to the concept of Haig than Liddell-Hart or Guderian. In the context of armour World War II unfolds as warfare with tanks rather than as tank warfare.

The introduction of any new weapon system is to a considerable degree a self-defeating process: in the case of the tank, its arrival sponsored the development of the anti-tank guns, mines, bazookas and tactical aircraft whose job was to produce a more hostile environment for it. Some pundits have even seen in this sequence a form of progression to a point at which the tank could become so vulnerable that it would cease to have any valid role at all. However, while it is true that the weapons introduced to counter the tank have all succeeded in showing that its armoured skin could be penetrated, a still more important factor to bear in mind is that armoured protection has never really been considered the tank's principal asset. This, first and foremost, has been its ability to provide a high degree of tactical mobility to heavy, crew-operated, direct-fire weapons; at the same time its armoured skin has afforded it protection from a significant number of battlefield weapons. It is this combination which accounted for the survival of

the tank during World War II and was the ultimate justification for its continued development in the post-war period.

At first the fortunes of the tank in Western armies suffered a decline. In the atmosphere of general euphoria at the end of the war, to which was joined a mystical belief in the power of the nuclear weapon, armoured divisions were disbanded at an alarming rate. However, the Western Alliance was shaken out of its complacency when Soviet T-34/85s, deployed by only moderately skilled North Koreans, wrought havoc among the infantry units of South Korea and the United States in June 1950. The mobile phase of the Korean War lasted until the summer of 1951 and the United Nations was forced to deploy tanks of World War II vintage, the American Pershing and the British Comet. It is ironic, too, that when the new tanks – Pattons and Centurions – did reach the theatre they were deployed in support of infantry in the slogging trench warfare that lasted until the ceasefire of June 1953. Yet the Korean War is an important episode in the story of the tank because it reawakened an interest in armour in the Western Alliance and accelerated the gun and armour race with the Soviet Union. This confrontation has, furthermore, taken place on a global scale with both sides liberally distributing their latest tanks to client and satellite powers which in turn have used them to fight their own wars in Asia and the Middle East.

OPPOSITE *Principal opponents in the Korean War (1950–53) were the Soviet-built T-34/85 (top), which were used to great effect early on by the North Koreans, and the American Patton and British*

Centurion (centre and bottom) with which the United Nations force eventually responded after the relative failure in the initial phase of its Pershings and Comets of World War II vintage.

ABOVE *A UN Sherman operating beside a burning farmhouse in Korea in 1950.* BELOW *A present-day tank position manned by South Korean soldiers and guarding the south bank of the Imjin River.*

An Israeli Sherman advancing into Syria during the 1967 campaign.

The Arab-Israeli Wars

The almost permanent nature of the quarrel between Arab and Jew has provided a ready-made testing ground for the tank and other armoured fighting vehicles. The Sinai campaign of 1956 offered little of value since the outmoded machines and old-fashioned tactics that were used did little to change the art of tank warfare. The 1967 campaign, however, was far more important since it provided the arena for the first large-scale collision of Western and Soviet tanks of modern design.

In four days of fast-moving desert combat Israeli armour inflicted a decisive defeat on the numerically superior Egyptian tank formations. The Israeli Air Force in a pre-emptive strike gained mastery of the skies above Sinai and this allowed the armoured divisions great freedom of movement. But even more conclusive was the manifest superiority of the Israeli armour. The Army had re-equipped with new tanks, mostly Pattons and Centurions, and at first experienced many difficulties in handling their

complex machines. In border clashes with Syria in 1965 the Arab Panzer Mark IVs proved more than a match for the Israelis and this resulted in a crisis of confidence in the Israeli Armoured Corps.

General Tal was appointed chief of the armoured forces and immediately carried through a major reform of his units. By 1967 the armoured divisions had been completely reformed and their popular image of a 'civilianized' bunch of freedom fighters was far removed from reality. The tank formations were an élite corps of well-drilled, disciplined troopers with a standard training programme, and although they were still largely composed of militia Tal had ensured that there was also a strong base of long-term regulars.

The tank campaign in Sinai was essentially a clash between the classic Soviet concepts of defence and the Israeli version of Guderian's Blitzkrieg. The Tal armoured divisions shocked the Egyptians into flight and then kept them on the run until they were exhausted; once through

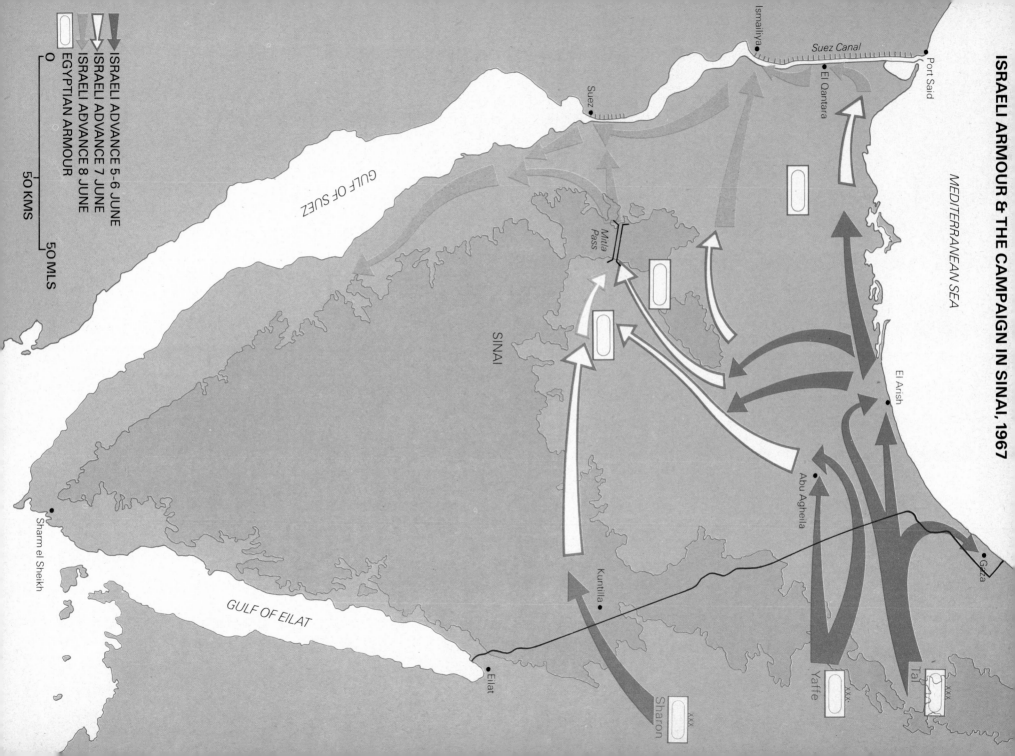

ISRAELI ARMOUR & THE CAMPAIGN IN SINAI, 1967

ISRAELI ADVANCE 5-6 JUNE
ISRAELI ADVANCE 7 JUNE
ISRAELI ADVANCE 8 JUNE
EGYPTIAN ARMOUR

0
50 KMS
50 MLS

MEDITERRANEAN SEA

Port Said
Ismailiya
Suez Canal
El Qantara
Suez
GULF OF SUEZ
Mitla Pass
SINAI
El Arish
Gaza
Abu Agheila
Tal
Yaffe
Kuntilla
GULF OF EILAT
Eilat
Sharm el Sheikh
Sharon

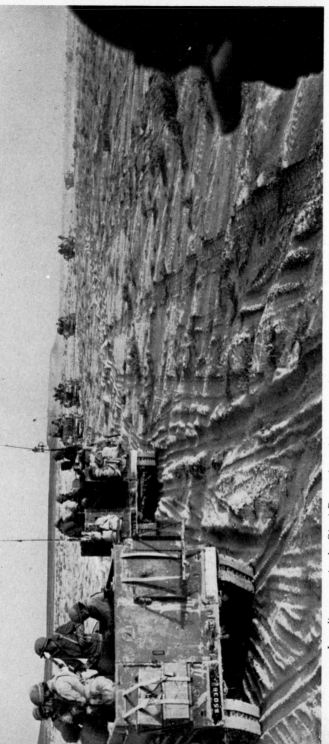

ABOVE *Israeli armour in the Sinai Desert in 1967.*

the first line of defences the Israeli tanks deployed to meet the main force of Egyptian armour. If the Arabs had fought with more resolution within their fortified positions, or if their Air Force had not been so effectively neutralized, then the cavalry charge by the Israeli tanks might well have stalled on the Egyptian wire. There were some very good combat units in the Egyptian Army, but they were the exception; in general the Egyptians' Russian instructors had had scant success in training their pupils in the complexities of a European-style tank war.

There is little documented evidence available on this lightning campaign: the Arabs are understandably reticent while Israeli information tends to mislead rather than inform. But although the details of this campaign remain obscure it appears that the Israelis attacked with three armoured divisions and achieved a major rupture of the Egyptian positions within the first 24 hours. During this first phase some of the heaviest fighting occurred, and the Egyptian minefields and artillery took a heavy toll of the advancing tanks. In the north General Tal 'pinched off' the Gaza Strip but then became embroiled in a large-scale fire-fight against the main Egyptian position astride the Ismalia Road. These forces were saved from further punishment when General Yaffe, who had struck largely unnoticed in the centre, was able to sweep northwards to rescue his leader. General Sharon and his division in the south had a tough battle against well-entrenched Egyptian units at Abu Aghelia, but a daring night assault through the minefields cleared the last of the defences and he moved south and west without pause for re-supply. The crucial

tank encounters occurred on a wide front throughout the second and third days, when the Egyptian T-54s and T-55s proved no match for the technically superior Israeli tanks. The Arab tank formations were either outflanked or destroyed piecemeal as the Israeli armour raced for the vital Mitla Pass and the road to the Suez Canal.

The great levelling factor in previous campaigns involving fast-moving armour had been the problem of supply, and in the present case war broke out before General Tal had been able to effect any genuine reform of the supply echelons of his tank formations. Hastily impressed lorries and their undisciplined drivers created massive traffic jams on the roads into Sinai and this self-inflicted strangulation meant that very few tanks were able to deploy in the Mitla Pass. Tanks with any fuel in store towed others which were bone-dry into blocking positions and so they were able to deny the pass to the retreating Egyptians until relief came. Air strikes also played a major role in the desert battle in the last three days of combat, and although the use of napalm by the Israelis meant that pinpoint accuracy was no longer required, very few Egyptian tanks were in fact 'killed' by air strikes. The real impact of the Israeli Air Force was felt in the massive destruction of supply echelons that took place as the Egyptian convoys tried to run for cover.

Much has been written about this campaign and the equally impressive operations against the Jordanians and Syrians, and some pundits of air power and the tank have performed incredible feats of academic gymnastics in trying to demonstrate new lessons. But the plain fact is that nothing new came out of that last cavalry ride to glory

Balance of Forces
ARAB/ISRAELI WAR JUNE 1967

CATEGORY	ISRAEL	EGYPT
1 Total armed forces	71,000 regulars (275,000 including reservists)	190,000 regulars (310,000 including reservists/national guard)
2 Army	60,000 regulars (204,000 including reservists)	160,000 regulars plus reservists
	Equipped with: 600 front-line tanks 200 Shermans 250 self-propelled guns	Equipped with: 1,200 tanks and self-propelled guns, the former consisting mainly of T-34/85, T-54, T-55, Centurion and AMX-13 tanks
3 Air Force	350 combat aircraft, including the Mirage IIIC, Super Mystère and Vautour	550 combat aircraft, including MiG-15, -19 and -21 interceptors

in a campaign which simply transported us back 25 years. The battle was won by a disciplined, technologically skilled nation that was able to defeat a well-equipped but badly-led army which apparently lacked the educational and social framework to fight a machine-age war.

In October 1973 the desert wastes of Sinai, still littered with the rusting hulks of the June 1967 war, witnessed a new clash of armour that took a different course. The war in fact began on two fronts: while élite Egyptian mechanized forces stormed the Bar-Lev Line on the east bank of the Suez canal, to the north Syrian tanks in massed formations advanced against complacent, and thinly held, Israeli outposts along the Golan Heights.

For 20 days the armoured units of both sides fought a series of bloody tank battles in a classic style: only on this occasion there was no Israeli Blitzkrieg to shock the Arab armies into premature flight. Instead it was the turn of the Arabs to confound the pundits as their tank regiments and supporting infantry fought with great skill and professionalism.

The Israelis' strategy soon became clear. This was to give priority to the Northern Front and so quell the danger there before counter-attacking in the south. But in the field their tactics were compromised by an overriding need to keep casualties to an acceptable minimum. In late October, with the Northern Front stabilized into an artillery duel and the Syrian forces pushed back to their start lines, an Israeli tank force burst through the Egyptian lines in the south and seized a bridgehead on the west bank of the Canal. Although the Israelis were able to expand their bridgehead and encircle the Egyptian Third Corps in and around the town of Suez, they were eventually stopped by a ceasefire, brought about by concerted pres-

ABOVE The French light AMX-13 tank, with which some Egyptian units were equipped.
BELOW Now a museum piece – a Russian-built SU-100 in Egyptian markings.

sure from the Great Powers and the UN, from completing the operation.

Throughout the campaign the Egyptians used new tactics. In the air the Israeli tactical strike aircraft found themselves inhibited by the accuracy of the Egyptians' surface-to-air missiles (mostly of the SAM-6 type), while on the ground the Egyptians matched their infantry against Israeli tanks and their own armour against Israeli infantry. That they were able to do so was in part due to the large stocks of wire-guided Sagger anti-tank missiles available to the infantry.

In this war more tanks were apparently destroyed than in any of the previous encounters, and this once again, predictably enough, resulted in experts forecasting the end of the battle tank. But the casualties, though high, were suffered primarily because both sides used tanks on such a large scale; the figures nevertheless also underline the effectiveness of tank cannon in the hands of confident and skilled crewmen.

OPPOSITE *In between wars — Israeli tank reservists on exercise in the desert. THIS PAGE Knocked-out Russian tanks with Arab markings in 1967 (above) and 1973 (lower picture).*

The Indo-Pakistan Wars

A pattern similar to that of the Arab–Israeli wars emerged when the Pakistanis and Indians clashed in 1965 and again in 1971. The western border war in 1965 provided the experts with a unique opportunity to assess the respective qualities of one Western tank against another as Pakistani Pattons tangled with Indian Centurions. But sterile tactics on both sides blunted this contest and produced a short, savage war of attrition in which neither side possessed the resilience to pursue matters beyond an indefinite conclusion. The advanced weapon systems that were used cancelled one another out very quickly, and if the Centurion emerged with its reputation more intact than the Patton, this was probably because it was far less sophisticated and much easier to handle.

The unsatisfactory truce achieved through Russian arbitration at Tashkent resulted in an uneasy lull, and open conflict, this time on a wider scale, erupted in 1971. The main centre of interest was focused on the eastern frontiers as both sides became embroiled in the birth pangs of secessionist Bangladesh. Little documentary evidence has emerged from this recent campaign but the accepted Indian version of events relates how within a brief period of twelve days their armoured columns executed one of the most decisive campaigns of liberation in military history. The largely infantry-orientated Pakistani forces in the east based their defences on a number of seemingly impregnable strategically located strongholds covering the lines of best approach. Indian armour moved across ground hitherto

considered inaccessible to tanks and outwitted an already demoralized enemy by swift outflanking movements.

The success of the Indian armour during this campaign confounded the image that experts in the Western world had formed of the Indian Army. But the construction under licence in India of a modified version of the Vickers battle tank (renamed the Vijayanta), added to their existing aircraft industry, made the Indians surprisingly self-sufficient for a developing nation. The London *Sunday Times*, in an article published on 19 December 1971, said:

It took only twelve days for the Indian Army to smash its way to Dacca, an achievement reminiscent of the German Blitzkrieg across France in 1940. The strategy was the same, speed, ferocity and flexibility.

On the western frontiers the Pakistanis launched major offensives to try and divert Indian forces from the major operations in the east. This stratagem failed and though the fighting in the west proved less decisive the Indians made some territorial gains by straightening out salients which had been created in 1965. Heavy fighting in this sector lasted until 17 December. The biggest tank battle occurred in the Shakargarh salient where Indian Army Centurions of the Poona Horse clashed with the Pakistani 6th Armour Division's Pattons, which contained elements of Hobson's Horse and Skinner's Horse. As the names themselves suggest, the irony of this particular encounter was that all these regiments had once been eminent cavalry formations in the British Indian Army.

Balance of Forces
INDO/PAKISTANI WAR DECEMBER 1971

CATEGORY		INDIA	PAKISTAN
1 Total armed forces		960,000 men	395,000 men
2 Army		840,000	278,000
[a] *Armoured formations*		2 armoured divisions	2 armoured divisions
		3 independent armoured brigades	1 independent armoured brigade
	Equipped with:	Equipped with:	Equipped with:
		200 Centurions (Mks 5/7)	135 M-47 Pattons
		250 Shermans	65 M-48 Pattons
		450 T-54s, T-55s	50 T-55s
		300 Vijayantas	200 T-59s
		150 PT-76s	200 light tanks
		140 AMX-13s	
[b] *Infantry formations*		13 infantry divisions	10 infantry divisions
		10 mountain divisions	
		6 independent infantry brigades	
		2 parachute brigades	
3 Air Force		650 combat aircraft	Not available

OPPOSITE *The Vickers battle tank, built under licence in India as the Vijayanta, was a key element in the 1971 war.* BELOW LEFT *Three Pakistani soldiers pose for the world's press with an Indian tank captured in the Kashmir.* BELOW RIGHT *Arms, ammunition and documents siezed by Indian forces as Pakistani troops fled from Bangladesh.*

Armour Today

The contribution of armour to the fighting in Vietnam is difficult to assess as a whole but it does seem that many valuable lessons have been learned, some of which have already been applied to the European theatre. For a number of years the Americans, their allies and clients have made good use of armoured personnel carriers – vehicles which have fulfilled the role of the light tank, whose virtues were so mistakenly espoused by Liddell-Hart and the British in the period from 1918 to 1939. The main battle tank made its appearance in the theatre only in the final phase of the war after 1968.

The Armoured Branch of the US Army advocated the use of tanks in the first instance because it believed that future tank development would be jeopardized unless the tank could draw at least some of the limelight away from the infantry. But, aside from this partisan motive, the tank was also needed by the Army Command to provide support for the infantry during this latter period of large-scale combat, when casualties were at their highest. Yet in a counter-insurgency operation the use of armour can have little value since the guerrilla is too elusive an objective for the tank and a sophisticated armoured thrust is hardly the most appropriate way to attack his primitive lines of communication, which can be easily reassembled.

The war in Vietnam caused a reformation in the research and development of conventional weapon systems – activities which had lain dormant in Europe since the end of World War II. In the context of armour the weapon which has aroused the greatest interest and controversy is the helicopter. In Vietnam helicopters performed a variety of tasks but they were at their most spectacular as a weapons carrier: on many occasions their ability to pour plunging fire of great density and little discrimination caused havoc among those caught in open country or confined in a village street. In terms of Europe it is this aspect of the helicopter, especially when converted to the role of tank killer, that has aroused the most interest and speculation; and there are some experts who predict the demise of the battle tank because of its vulnerability to the helicopter. The modern helicopter can carry a lethal missile that can be fired at a range of four kilometres – well beyond the range of any tank's defending fire. The great speed and manoeuvrability of the helicopter mean that it is also able rapidly to bring reinforcement to a situation of crisis on a modern battle-field; it is this factor above all which many observers find so attractive.

The modern battle tanks of three nations.
ABOVE The US M-60, in effect a diesel-
engined M-48 (the Mark III Patton)
mounting the British-designed 105-mm
gun; the A-1 E-1 version of the M-60
mounts the Shillelagh gun/guided missile.
BELOW The MBT-70, shown with its
suspension fully depressed; this US-West
German co-venture was cancelled
because of ever-mounting costs.
OPPOSITE, ABOVE The AMX-30, the
French main battle tank mounting a
105-mm gun; it has infra-red driving and
fire-control equipment and can be fitted
with a snorkel for deep-wading. Variants
include a bridgelayer, a recovery vehicle
and the Pluton missile carrier.
OPPOSITE, BELOW The medium Leopard,
a 40-mph West German tank armed with a
105-mm gun. Variants include armoured
recovery and anti-aircraft vehicles.

In the future few changes are likely in the shape and design of armoured formations within the Western Alliance. The Americans and the West Germans cancelled their joint project, called the MBT-70, because of rapidly escalating costs. The Americans for a while flirted with a tank project of advanced design known as the XM-803 but have now abandoned this in favour of a more modest project. The West Germans plan to improve on the Leopard while at the same time co-operating with Britain on a joint project for a battle tank that is scheduled at the time of writing to replace existing equipment by the end of the decade.

Two other countries outside the main Alliance have recently developed main battle tanks. One of these, Sweden, has the S tank, built by Bofors; this vehicle is of a revolutionary design and shape but is regarded by many purists as a super-self-propelled gun, rather than a tank. The other country, Japan, showed only slight interest in armour during World War II, but now, in modest quantities, she possesses a battle tank called the Type 61. This tank, however, shares so many similarities with the American Patton that one wonders why the Japanese bothered to build their own.

At the present time the emphasis placed on tanks by the major armies of the world reflects the continuing validity of armoured vehicles to the modern battlefield despite the accelerating development of anti-tank weapons. However, in a European context the tank can no longer be deployed as cavalry; armoured divisions will never again lie massed in reserve to exploit a fractured battle front. The tactical nuclear weapon has shrunk the battlefield, inhibited the mobility of the tank, and placed a fresh emphasis on the need for systematic destruction through the use of overwhelming firepower. In 1971 *The Economist* (London) said:

The tank for a long period has been the king of European warfare – indeed for most people it has become the symbol of armed might and coercion; now it looks as if it has been dethroned from supreme power.

The future of tanks has been questioned many times and for the most part the conclusions reached have suggested that their end was at hand. In the past tanks have been written off because of the development of new armour-piercing weapons. This happened in the 1930s with the arrival of small-calibre anti-tank guns and again in World War II when experts pointed to the destructive capabilities of the rocket-firing Stuka aircraft and to the infantry bazooka. And in the present-day period guided heli-borne missiles are seen by many as the instruments most likely to determine the fate of the tank.

Certainly, such weapons have all proved that the armour protection of the tank can be penetrated. But this is no reason to dismiss its value on the battlefield; tanks have never been immune to hostile fire and armour protection has never been considered their principal asset.

Thus all conclusions that tanks are liable to be made obsolete by new anti-tank weapons are logical – but are derived from a false premise. For the principal asset of the tank is, as we stated earlier, its ability to provide a high degree of tactical mobility to heavy, direct-fire weapons. This simple fact accounts for the tank's survival despite its increasing vulnerability – and also explains why it is likely to continue to be developed for many years ahead.

Shown on these pages are three views of a remarkable vehicle, the Swedish S or Stridsvagn tank, built by Bofors. Its revolutionary design, with ultra-low profile, places considerable — some critics would say undue — emphasis on the fixed

main armament, a 105-mm gun. For to fire it, the whole of the vehicle has to be hydraulically swung onto the target, which means that the gun can only be used provided all the machine's numerous other components are in sound working order

(hardly ideal, perhaps, for combat conditions). However, whether it is a tank or a super self-propelled gun, the main armament can fire at the rapid rate of 10–15 rounds per minute. The S tank has a crew of three.

DATA SECTION
1: Details of Important Tanks

Table 1 : Details of important tanks

The statistical information in this table has been gathered from many sources, among which variations occur. The figures given here are those which seemed to the author and the editors most likely to be accurate. The category 'length (overall)' includes any part of the main gun overhanging the front of the tank.

'Range' refers to the longest distance a tank can cover on level road on one filling of fuel; in cross-country movement a tank's range is always considerably reduced, usually by 20–30 per cent., though the precise amount varies according to the vehicle and the conditions in which it operates.

World War I

MARK I Male
(Britain) 1916

Length	32 feet 6 inches (with tail)
Width	13 feet 9 inches
Height	8 feet 0 inches
Weight	28 tons
Speed	3·7 mph (max.)
Range	23·6 miles
Armament	2 × 57-mm (6-pounder) guns with 332 rounds
	4 machine-guns with 6,272 rounds
Armour	10 mm (max. thickness)
Crew	8

ST CHAMOND Char d'assaut
(France) 1916

Length	26 feet 6 inches (overall)
Width	8 feet 11 inches
Height	7 feet 10 inches
Weight	23 tons
Speed	5 mph (max.)
Range	37 miles
Armament	1 × 75-mm gun with 106 rounds
	4 × 7·92-mm machine-guns with 7,488 rounds
Armour	17 mm (max. thickness)
Crew	8

MARK V Male
(Britain) 1918

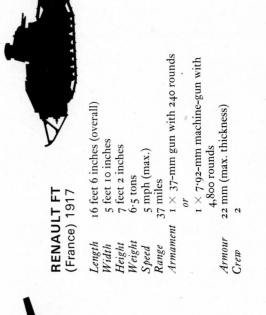

Length	26 feet 5 inches (overall)
Width	12 feet 9 inches
Height	8 feet 8 inches
Weight	29 tons
Speed	4·6 mph (max.)
Range	45 miles
Armament	2 × 57-mm (6-pounder) guns with 207 rounds
	4 machine-guns with 5,700 rounds
Armour	12 mm (max. thickness)
Crew	8

RENAULT FT
(France) 1917

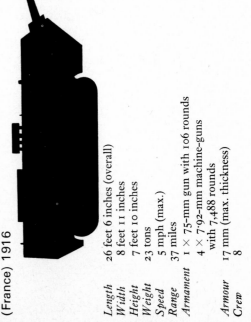

Length	16 feet 6 inches (overall)
Width	5 feet 10 inches
Height	7 feet 2 inches
Weight	6·5 tons
Speed	5 mph (max.)
Range	37 miles
Armament	1 × 37-mm gun with 240 rounds
	or
	1 × 7·92-mm machine-gun with 4,800 rounds
Armour	22 mm (max. thickness)
Crew	2

Inter-War Period

MEDIUM A WHIPPET
(Britain) 1918

Length	20 feet 0 inches (overall)
Width	8 feet 7 inches
Height	9 feet 0 inches
Weight	14 tons
Speed	8·3 mph (max.)
Range	80 miles
Armament	4 machine-guns with 5,400 rounds
Armour	14 mm (max. thickness)
Crew	3

VICKERS MEDIUM MARK II
(Britain) 1927

Length	17 feet 6 inches (overall)
Width	9 feet 2 inches
Height	9 feet 3 inches
Weight	12·5 tons
Speed	15 mph (max.)
Range	150 miles
Armament	1 × 47-mm (3-pounder) gun
	6 × ·303-inch machine-guns
Armour	8 mm (max. thickness)
Crew	5

CHAR B
(France) 1931

Length	21 feet 9 inches (overall)
Width	8 feet 3 inches
Height	9 feet 4 inches
Weight	31 tons
Speed	17 mph (max.)
Range	125 miles
Armament	1 × 75-mm howitzer with 74 rounds
	1 × 37-mm gun with 75 rounds
	2 × 7·5-mm machine-guns with 5,100 rounds
Armour	60 mm (max. thickness)
Crew	4

BT-5
(USSR) 1933

Length	18 feet 2 inches (overall)
Width	7 feet 2 inches
Height	7 feet 8 inches
Weight	11·5 tons
Speed	38 mph (max.)
Range	112 miles
Armament	1 × 45-mm gun with 115 rounds
	1 × 7·62-mm machine-gun with 2,500 rounds
Armour	13 mm (max. thickness)
Crew	3

PZKW MARK IA
(Germany) 1934

Length	13 feet 2 inches (overall)
Width	6 feet 10 inches
Height	5 feet 8 inches
Weight	5·4 tons
Speed	22 mph (max.)
Range	90 miles
Armament	2 × 7·92-mm machine-guns with 3,050 rounds
Armour	13 mm (max. thickness)
Crew	2

VICKERS LIGHT MARK VI
(Britain) 1935

Length	13 feet 2 inches (overall)
Width	6 feet 9 inches
Height	7 feet 3 inches
Weight	5·2 tons
Speed	29 mph (max.)
Range	125 miles
Armament	1 × ·303-inch machine-gun with 2,500 rounds
	1 × ·5-inch machine-gun with 400 rounds
Armour	14 mm (max. thickness)
Crew	3

A-10 CRUISER MARK IIA
(Britain) 1935

Length	18 feet 1 inch (overall)
Width	8 feet 3 inches
Height	8 feet 6 inches
Weight	14 tons
Speed	15 mph (max.)
Range	100 miles
Armament	1 × 40-mm (2-pounder) gun
	2 × 7·92-mm machine-guns
Armour	30 mm (max. thickness)
Crew	5

KV-I
(USSR) 1939

Length	22 feet 6 inches (overall)
Width	11 feet 0 inches
Height	9 feet 0 inches
Weight	43·5 tons
Speed	25 mph (max.)
Range	210 miles
Armament	1 × 76·2-mm gun with 111 rounds
	3 × 7·62-mm machine-guns with 3,000 rounds
Armour	90 mm (max. thickness)
Crew	5

CRUSADER CRUISER MARK I
(Britain) 1939

Length	19 feet 7 inches (overall)
Width	9 feet 1 inch
Height	7 feet 4 inches
Weight	18·5 tons
Speed	27 mph (max.)
Range	200 miles
Armament	1 × 40-mm (2-pounder) gun with 110 rounds
	2 × 7·92-mm machine-guns with 4,500 rounds
Armour	40 mm (max. thickness)
Crew	5

STUART M-3 MARK I
(USA) 1940

Length	14 feet 10 inches (overall)
Width	7 feet 4 inches
Height	8 feet 3 inches
Weight	12·25 tons
Speed	37 mph (max.)
Range	100 miles
Armament	1 × 37-mm gun with 103 rounds
	3 machine-guns
Armour	38 mm (max. thickness)
Crew	4

M-13/40
(Italy) 1940

Length	16 feet 2 inches
Width	7 feet 3 inches
Height	7 feet 4 inches
Weight	14 tons
Speed	20 mph (max.)
Range	125 miles
Armament	1 × 47-mm gun
	3 machine-guns
Armour	40 mm (max. thickness)
Crew	4

MATILDA INFANTRY MARK II
(Britain) 1938

Length	18 feet 5 inches (overall)
Width	8 feet 3 inches
Height	7 feet 10 inches
Weight	26 tons
Speed	15 mph (max.)
Range	60 miles
Armament	1 × 40-mm (2-pounder) gun
	1 × 7·92-mm machine-gun
Armour	80 mm (max. thickness)
Crew	4

PZKW MARK IIIA
(Germany) 1938

Length	18 feet 11 inches (overall)
Width	9 feet 4 inches
Height	7 feet 9 inches
Weight	15 tons
Speed	20 mph (max.)
Range	100 miles
Armament	1 × 37-mm gun with 150 rounds
	3 × 7·92-mm machine-guns with 4,500 rounds
Armour	14·5 mm (max. thickness)
Crew	5

T-34/76A
(USSR) 1939

Length	21 feet 7 inches (overall)
Width	9 feet 10 inches
Height	8 feet 0 inches
Weight	28 tons
Speed	32 mph (max.)
Range	190 miles
Armament	1 × 76·2-mm gun with 76 rounds
	2 × 7·62-mm machine-guns with 2,900 rounds
Armour	45 mm (max. thickness)
Crew	4

GRANT MEDIUM M-3 (USA) 1941

Length: 18 feet 6 inches (overall)
Width: 8 feet 11 inches
Height: 10 feet 4 inches
Weight: 29 tons
Speed: 26 mph
Range: 160 miles
Armament:
1 × 75-mm gun with 46 rounds
1 × 37-mm gun with 178 rounds
4 × 3-inch machine-guns with 9,200 rounds
Armour: 57 mm (max. thickness)
Crew: 6

PZKW MARK IVE (Germany) 1941

Length: 19 feet 8½ inches (overall)
Width: 9 feet 6½ inches
Height: 8 feet 11 inches
Weight: 21 tons
Speed: 27 mph (max.)
Range: 125 miles
Armament:
1 × 75-mm gun with 87 rounds
2 × 7·92-mm machine-guns with 2,700 rounds
Armour: 60 mm (max. thickness)
Crew: 5

PANTHER D (Germany) 1942

Length: 29 feet 6 inches (overall)
Width: 11 feet 5 inches
Height: 9 feet 10 inches
Weight: 43 tons
Speed: 28 mph (max.)
Range: 105 miles
Armament:
1 × 75-mm gun with 79 rounds
1 × 7·92-mm machine-gun with 4,200 rounds
Armour: 80 mm (max. thickness)
Crew: 5

T-34/85 (USSR) 1942

Length: 24 feet 9 inches (overall)
Width: 9 feet 10 inches
Height: 7 feet 11 inches
Weight: 32 tons
Speed: 32 mph (max.)
Range: 190 miles
Armament:
1 × 85-mm gun with 55 rounds
2 × 7·62-mm machine-guns with 2,745 rounds
Armour: 75 mm (max. thickness)
Crew: 5

SHERMAN MARK V (USA) 1942

Length: 21 feet 6 inches (overall)
Width: 8 feet 9 inches
Height: 9 feet 5 inches
Weight: 33 tons
Speed: 25 mph (max.)
Range: 100 miles
Armament:
1 × 75-mm gun
2 machine-guns
Armour: 85 mm (max. thickness)
Crew: 5

TIGER MARK IE (Germany) 1942

Length: 27 feet 5 inches (overall)
Width: 12 feet 6 inches
Height: 9 feet 6 inches
Weight: 56 tons
Speed: 24 mph (max.)
Range: 62 miles
Armament:
1 × 88-mm gun with 92 rounds
2 × 7·92-mm machine-guns with 3,920 rounds
Armour: 100 mm (max. thickness)
Crew: 5

CHURCHILL MARK II (Britain) 1942

Length: 24 feet 5 inches (overall)
Width: 10 feet 8 inches
Height: 8 feet 2 inches
Weight: 38·5 tons
Speed: 17 mph (max.)
Range: 90 miles
Armament:
1 × 40-mm (2-pounder) gun
2 × 7·92-mm machine-guns
Armour: 102 mm (max. thickness)
Crew: 5

CROMWELL MARK IV (Britain) 1944

Length: 20 feet 10 inches (overall)
Width: 9 feet 7 inches
Height: 8 feet 3 inches
Weight: 28 tons
Speed: 38 mph (max.)
Range: 165 miles
Armament:
1 × 75-mm gun with 64 rounds
2 × 7·92-mm machine-guns with 4,950 rounds
Armour: 76 mm (max. thickness)
Crew: 5

JS-III (USSR) 1944

Length	32 feet 9 inches (overall)
Width	10 feet 6 inches
Height	8 feet 10 inches
Weight	46 tons
Speed	23 mph (max.)
Range	130 miles
Armament	1 × 122-mm gun with 28 rounds
	2 × 7·62-mm machine-guns
	1 × 12·7-mm machine-gun
Armour	230 mm (max. thickness)
Crew	4

COMET (Britain) 1945

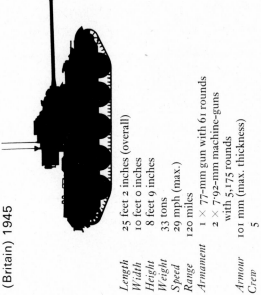

Length	25 feet 2 inches (overall)
Width	10 feet 0 inches
Height	8 feet 9 inches
Weight	33 tons
Speed	29 mph (max.)
Range	120 miles
Armament	1 × 77-mm gun with 61 rounds
	2 × 7·92-mm machine-guns with 5,175 rounds
Armour	101 mm (max. thickness)
Crew	5

PERSHING M-26 (USA) 1945

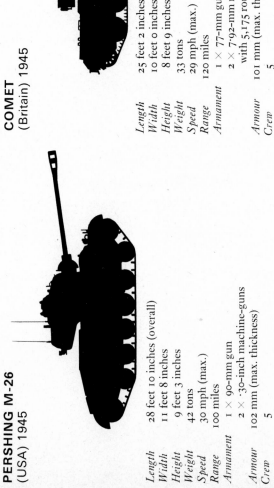

Length	28 feet 10 inches (overall)
Width	11 feet 8 inches
Height	9 feet 3 inches
Weight	42 tons
Speed	30 mph (max.)
Range	100 miles
Armament	1 × 90-mm gun
	2 × ·30-inch machine-guns
Armour	102 mm (max. thickness)
Crew	5

Post-1945 Period

CENTURION MARK 3 (Britain) 1948

Length	32 feet 3 inches (overall)
Width	11 feet 1 inch
Height	9 feet 8 inches
Weight	49 tons
Speed	22 mph (max.)
Range	85 miles
Armament	1 × 83·4-mm (20-pounder) gun with 65 rounds
	1 × 7·92-mm machine-gun with 3,600 rounds
Armour	152 mm (max. thickness)
Crew	4

AMX-13 (France) 1949

Length	20 feet 9 inches (overall)
Width	8 feet 3 inches
Height	7 feet 4 inches
Weight	14·7 tons
Speed	40 mph (max.)
Range	205 miles
Armament	1 × 75-mm gun with 40 rounds
	1 × 7·5-mm machine-gun with 3,000 rounds
Armour	40 mm (max. thickness)
Crew	3

PATTON M-47
(USA) 1949

Length	27 feet 9 inches (overall)
Width	11 feet 6 inches
Height	9 feet 8 inches
Weight	44 tons
Speed	35 mph (max.)
Range	75 miles
Armament	1 × 90-mm gun with 71 rounds
	2 × 12·7-mm machine-guns
	1 × 7·62-mm machine-gun
Armour	115 mm (max. thickness)
Crew	5

T-54A
(USSR) 1954

Length	29 feet 6 inches (overall)
Width	10 feet 9 inches
Height	7 feet 10 inches
Weight	36 tons
Speed	34 mph (max.)
Range	210 miles
Armament	1 × 100-mm gun with 42 rounds
	1 × 12·7-mm machine-gun with 500 rounds
	2 × 7·62-mm machine-guns with 3,000 rounds
Armour	105 mm (max. thickness)
Crew	4

T-62
(USSR) 1963

Length	31 feet 0 inches (overall)
Width	11 feet 0 inches
Height	7 feet 4 inches
Weight	37 tons
Speed	34 mph (max.)
Range	190 miles
Armament	1 × 115-mm gun with 45 rounds
	1 × 7·62-mm machine-gun with 2,200 rounds
Armour	100 mm (max. thickness)
Crew	4

LEOPARD
(West Germany) 1965

Length	31 feet 0 inches (overall)
Width	10 feet 7 inches
Height	7 feet 10 inches
Weight	40 tons
Speed	42 mph (max.)
Range	310 miles
Armament	1 × 105-mm gun with 60 rounds
	2 × 7·62-mm machine-guns
Armour	–
Crew	4

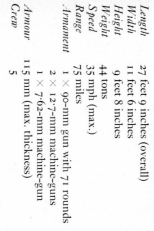

AMX-30
(France) 1966

Length	30 feet 3 inches (overall)
Width	10 feet 3 inches
Height	8 feet 2 inches
Weight	34 tons
Speed	40 mph (max.)
Range	350 miles
Armament	1 × 105-mm gun with 56 rounds
	1 × 12·7-mm machine-gun with 600 rounds
	1 × 7·62-mm machine-gun with 1,600 rounds
Armour	–
Crew	4

M-60 A-1
(USA) 1961

Length	30 feet 11 inches (overall)
Width	11 feet 11 inches
Height	10 feet 4 inches
Weight	46 tons
Speed	35 mph (max.)
Range	300 miles
Armament	1 × 105-mm gun with 63 rounds
	3 machine-guns
Armour	110 mm (est. max. thickness)
Crew	4

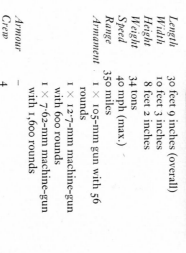

S-TANK
(Sweden) 1967

Length	29 feet 4 inches (overall)
Width	10 feet 11 inches
Height	7 feet 0 inches
Weight	37 tons
Speed	30 mph (max.)
Range	200 miles
Armament	1 × 105-mm gun with 50 rounds
	2 × 7·62-mm machine-gun with 2,650 rounds
Armour	–
Crew	3

TYPE 61
(Japan) 1962

Length	27 feet 8 inches (overall)
Width	9 feet 8 inches
Height	7 feet 4 inches
Weight	34 tons
Speed	28 mph (max.)
Range	125 miles
Armament	1 × 90-mm gun
	1 × 12·7-mm machine-gun
	1 × 7·7-mm machine-gun
Armour	–
Crew	4

CHIEFTAIN MARK 2
(Britain) 1965

Length	35 feet 2 inches (overall)
Width	11 feet 6 inches
Height	9 feet 3 inches
Weight	51 tons
Speed	25 mph (max.)
Range	250 miles
Armament	1 × 120-mm gun with 53 rounds
	1 × 12·7-mm machine-gun with 600 rounds
	2 × 7·62-mm machine-guns with 6,000 rounds
Armour	–
Crew	4

The material most commonly, though by no means exclusively, used to armour tanks is heat-treated alloy steel. Among the many other materials that have proved suitable in the past and are employed today are alloys of aluminium, magnesium and titanium, and non-metallic metals such as plastic laminates and nylon fabric, concrete and mastic stone composites.

The steel armour first produced for tanks was generally of two types, homogeneous and face-hardened.

Face-hardened armour

This type of armour was specially processed to give a very hard, penetration-resistant surface layer on the face exposed to attack. A softer but tougher core supported the hardened surface.

This armour was especially effective against early types of armour-piercing projectiles in that the hardened surface caused the nose of the projectile to shatter, thereby defeating the projectile's principal aim of penetrating the target armour.

The next step followed the discovery, by naval experts, that thick, face-hardened armour could be defeated by making the noses of armour-piercing projectiles blunter, and by fitting them with soft steel caps which lessened the impact forces on the nose of the shot. By the beginning of World War II, steel-capped armour-piercing projectiles had, in fact, long been standard for naval use.

It was then a matter of applying this knowledge to land warfare. The Germans led the way, followed quickly by the Allied armies, and armour-piercing caps were fitted to anti-tank projectiles of all calibres. The new projectiles soon overcame the face-hardened armour opposed to them. As a result this type of armour, which was expensive and took a long time to manufacture, was generally abandoned for use on armoured vehicles at an early stage in the war.

Homogeneous armour

Homogeneous armour was of two kinds – wrought, or rolled, and cast. Of these the latter was the most popular. Steel armour casting was first employed for tanks in the early 1930s by the Germans, and the technique was perfected in the USA by 1933. With the advent of World War II there came an enormous expansion in tank production. It soon proved impossible to roll all the armour plate that was needed, and the steel castings industry was called upon to produce large, shaped castings.

By 1942, in the USA alone, tens of thousands of tons of steel armour castings were being produced each month for tank turrets, hull-front housings and other components.

Above a minimum thickness of 1½ inches, cast armour was the equal in ballistic qualities to rolled armour. Since, too, in the later years of the war, medium and heavy tanks carried armour from 2 to 6 inches thick, cast armour was generally favoured.

Armour protection

In addition to the considerations described above, the principal factors governing the degree of protection afforded by armour are its thickness and its angle of slope with respect to the line of fire. The thickness of armour is critical in determining the weight of vehicles, and throughout the tank's history its designers have had to choose between having *either* protection through weight of metal *or* mobility.

In real terms, steel armour 1 inch thick can weigh 41 pounds per square foot. Thus a covering of 1 inch of armour (suitable for a light tank) may contribute 10 tons to such a vehicle's weight.

A universal compromise in the weight/mobility predicament has been to opt for sloped armour. This offers two main advantages: first of all, highly sloped armour (say to an angle of 60°) can deflect shot; secondly, it lengthens the path through the armour of a penetrating projectile, thus absorbing much of the latter's energy. In short, a piece of angled armour affords greater protection than a thicker plate positioned at 90° to the line of fire.

It was also found that the best way to carry out highly sloped designs was by casting. By this method complete hulls and turrets could each be cast in one piece, while the thickness of the armour could be adjusted to provide thicker sections in the less highly sloped areas.

The table below illustrates the hull and turret armour dispositions of World War II tanks. It is generally representative of vehicles made by all the major belligerents.

Type of tank	Tank weight (tons)	FRONTAL ARMOUR Thickness (inches)	FRONTAL ARMOUR Angle of slope	SIDE ARMOUR Thickness (inches)
Light	15-20	1.0-1.5	45°-60°	0.75-1.0
Medium	25-45	2.0-4.0	50°-60°	1.5-2.0
Heavy	50-65	4.0-6.0	50°-70°	2.0-3.0

3: Five long serving Tanks

The table shows how a successful tank's career may extend – across a period of more than 20 years – and the many wars that usually occur in such a span. The lively Renault FT, produced in comparatively vast quantities at the beginning of her life, lasted from the middle of World War I until two years into World War II. The later tanks illustrated here – some of which are still operational – came to serve many masters in the shifting scene of conflicts since 1945; the variety of their battlefield appearances reflects the many-sided alliances made in recent years by the Great Powers.

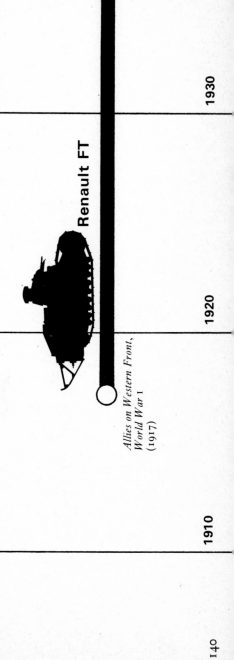

Renault FT

Allies on Western Front, World War 1 (1917)

1910 1920 1930

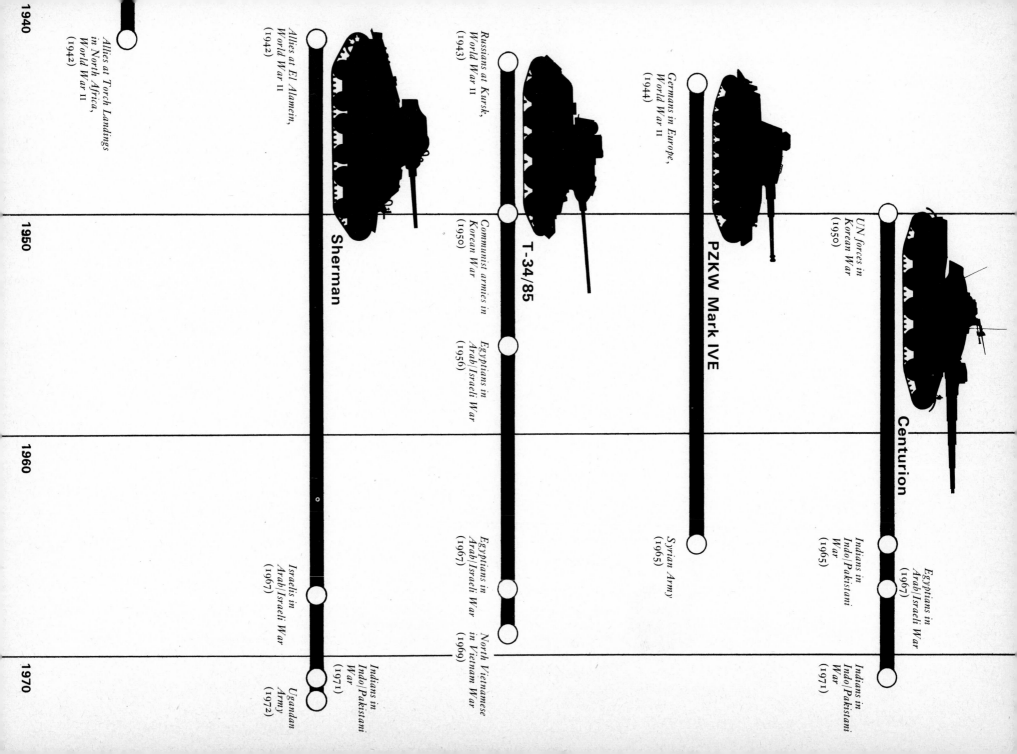

1940

1950

1960

1970

Allies at Torch Landings in North Africa, World War II (1942)

Allies at El Alamein, World War II (1942)

Sherman

Russians at Kursk, World War II (1943)

Communist armies in Korean War (1950)

Israelis in Arab/Israeli War (1967)

Ugandan Army (1972)

T-34/85

Egyptians in Arab/Israeli War (1956)

Egyptians in Arab/Israeli War (1967)

North Vietnamese in Vietnam War (1969)

Germans in Europe, World War II (1944)

PZKW Mark IVE

Syrian Army (1965)

UN forces in Korean War (1950)

Centurion

Indians in Indo/Pakistani War (1965)

Indians in Indo/Pakistani War (1971)

Egyptians in Arab/Israeli War (1967)

Indians in Indo/Pakistani War (1971)

4: Armour-piercing Projectiles of World War II

Three developments in anti-tank weapons rendered armour considerably more vulnerable to attack as World War II progressed.

The first came from improvements in anti-tank guns and their propellants, as a result of which muzzle velocities increased from approx. 2,000 feet per second in 1939 to 3,500 feet per second in 1945. This in turn produced a threefold increase in the ability of projectiles to penetrate their targets. The much vaunted German 88-mm gun was, for example, chiefly successful because its muzzle velocity (3,400 feet per second) was considerably ahead of its rivals.

The second development was the adoption (by the Germans, to begin with) of steel-capped armour-piercing projectiles. These had light outer cases and armour-piercing cores of tungsten carbide, an extremely hard substance almost twice the weight of steel. But because the total weight of these shells was less than that of the more conventional solid steel shot, they could be fired at higher muzzle velocities. Furthermore, only the relatively small core penetrated the target armour, and so a large amount of energy was applied to a small target area, which resulted in greater penetration.

The third development was the most potent of all. This was the 'shaped charge' or 'bazooka', first taken up by the Americans. This ammunition contained a charge of high explosive behind a conical metal liner. When the charge was detonated the liner was collapsed and projected forward as a narrow beam of extremely high-velocity incandescent particles. At short ranges this perforated armour in much the same way that a high-velocity water jet blows through an embankment of earth.

Tank defence tactics

Defence against the new threats to tank survival was for the most part a matter of on-the-spot improvisation. Some field workshops bolted additional thicknesses of armour to the fronts and turrets of tanks, and generally experimented with 'spaced-armour' arrangements with the object of reducing the impact of enemy projectiles on the main, inner layer of armour.

But on the whole it was left to individual crews to devise their own methods of protection. To this end sandbags, sections of spare track, tool-boxes, personal kit and other 'battle-expendable' gear came to be festooned around tanks in the hope that the enemy's projectiles would either be deflected or caused to function prematurely, i.e. before they struck the main armour.

5: Analysis of a Tank Mission

The chief task of a tank is successfully to destroy targets on the battlefield. And the principal criterion of a tank's tactical effectiveness is its ability to damage or destroy hostile tanks.

But before hostile armour can be destroyed, a number of independent events have to occur; on these the success of a mission depends. In the language of the professional strategist, the chain of events may be summarized in the following formula:

$$Pss = Pa \times Ps \times Pd \times Ph \times Pp \times Pl \times Pr$$

In other words, the probability of overall success (Pss) is the product of seven essential factors:

1 The tank has to be *available* at the appropriate time (**Pa**).

2 It must *survive* hostile activity long enough to launch its own attack (**Ps**).

3 The tank has to *detect* its target (**Pd**).

4 It must then succeed in *hitting* its target (**Ph**).

5 The hit must *penetrate* the target armour (**Pp**).

6 *Lethal* damage must be produced (**Pl**).

7 The above conditions are also subject to the whole offensive system functioning *reliably* (**Pr**).

These provisos perhaps demonstrate some of the recurring problems that face military planners and commanders in the field. They show, too, that the chances of battlefield success are not always as good as they may sometimes appear.

Index

Page numbers in *italics* refer to captions to illustrations and tabulated information.

Acknowledgments

The publishers would like to thank the following individuals and organizations for their kind permission to reproduce the pictures in this book:

Army Air Corps: 123 below; Associated Press: 52 both, 56 both, 99 below, 119 below, 123 above; Barratt's Photo Press Ltd. 111 above; A. B. Bofors: 130, 131 both; BPC Picture Library: 51 below; BPC Picture Library/Imperial War Museum: 62; Camera Press London: 1, 2–3, 8, 113 below, 118 below, 121 left; Central Office of Information, Photographs Division: 114, 118 above; Daily Telegraph Magazine: 116, 118 above, 119 above; C. M. Dixon: 10 above and below right; Fox Studios: 20 above; John

Hillelson Agency Ltd: 123 centre; Michael Holford: 10 left; Robert Hunt Library: 25 above, 29 above, 32, 33 below, 34 above, 39 both, 44 both, 47 above, 48 above, 50 below, 54 below, 57 below, 60, 68, 69 both, 70, 72 all, 73 both, 80, 81 below, 82 both, 83, 84, 85 both, 88 above, 89 above, 90, 91 both, 92 all, 93 above, 94 both, 96, 97 below right, 98 both, 99 above, 102 below, 103, 104 both, 105 both, 106 both, 107 above, 108 both, 110 above and below, 111 centre; Robert Hunt Library/Imperial War Museum: 22, 35 above; Imperial War Museum: 4–5, 14, 14–15, 34 below, 35 below, 64 below, 62, 65 above, 88 below left and right, 89 below; Keystone Press Agency: 43 above, 57 above, 109 both, 113 above, 121 right; Michael Leitch: 11 all; Mansell Collection 12; National Archives, Washington D.C.: 18; Novosti Press Agency: 13 above, 49 above and below right, 53 both, 96, 81 above, 93 below, 97

centre right, 124, 125 all; Popperfoto: 33 above, 46, 63, 65 centre, 102 above; RAC Tank Museum, Bovington: 20 below, 23 all, 40, 41 below, 49 top, 54 above, 65 below, 69 below, 107 below, 110 centre, 111 below, 112 all, 117 both, 128 both, 129 both; 'Soldier Magazine': 127 below; Staats Bibliothek, Berlin: 13 below; State of Israel Press Office: 116 above; Syndication International: 122; The Times: 43 below; H. Roger Viollet: 21 above and below, 24 all, 25 below, 28, 29 below, 55, 64, 140; Vickers Ltd: 47 below, 49 centre right, 50 above, 120; Jacket illustrations: (front) Centurion (John Rigby); (back) Sherman (Daily Telegraph Colour Library); Endpapers: Camera Press; The drawings on the front and back flaps and in the text were prepared specially for this book by Nigel Osborne, William Robertshaw and Arka Graphics. Extract on page 92 courtesy of Cassell & Co Ltd.